TALES OF AN IKUT SWAMI

CRISTINA KESSLER

To Joanne —

I hope you enjoy this celebration
of women @ the world. We can all
make a difference.

WOMEN ROCK!

Cristina Kessler

CRISTINA KESSLER

Book cover design by Frank Welffens
Photography by Cristina Kessler

ACKNOWLEDGEMENTS

There are many people to thank who have made this book possible. First of all, thanks to my true love Joe, who gave me a chance to travel the world, and make a difference in my own small ways. Thanks to Steve Katona who really encouraged me to write this book; thanks to all my women friends like Valerie Dickson-Horton and Paulette Nichols who I met in far-flung places as they dedicated their lives to making a difference; thanks to my mentor and inspiration, Patricia Lee Gauch, who started me on the author's path; thanks to my talented friend, Karen Jones Meadows who inspires me as an artist and compassionate soul; and thanks to my good friend Frank Welffens, the creator of and phenomenal web master who has made for me the world's greatest website and who formatted, designed and encouraged me every step of the way to produce TALES OF AN IKUT SWAMI.

And lastly, thanks to the women of the world, who would make it a safer and saner place if we were in charge. ALL OF YOU ROCK!

FOREWORD

Feasting on Cristina Kessler's cornucopia of cultural adventures is the perfect nourishment our connection-starved humanity craves. Her vivid, hilarious, cheer and tear inducing, wrenchingly honest recounts of traipsing throughout the world is at its core an exceptional husband wife love story, while a euphoric celebration of accidental and intentional bonding with diverse women resulting in unpredictable escapades and outcomes. A self-styled global ambassador with an iconoclastic flair and flare, Cristina's persistent bravery and willingness to delve into physical and emotional terrains most of us don't know exist, and if we do, avoid, is her hand holding offer to transcend our limited understanding of the preciousness of every person, and an invitation to embrace opportunities to live and give from the heart, changing the world one idea and one relationship at a time.

Karen Marie Jones Meadows

Karen Marie Jones Meadows is the writer and performer of a one-woman play, Harriet's Return: Based Upon the Legendary Life of Harriet Tubman.

CRISTINA KESSLER

TALES OF AN IKUT SWAMI

INTRODUCTION
St. John, Virgin Islands
2017

When I was 12 I was hit by a car while riding a bicycle. It was four days before beginning seventh grade and I was escorting my younger brother Brian on our bikes so he could get a haircut. One second we were racing along and the next I was on the hood of a car and looking through the windshield at three screaming guys. Once the car finally skidded to a halt I flew through the air and landed like a sack of potatoes on my head. I'll always remember leaving my body to watch in a circle of strangers as I quacked like a duck and spasmed in the road. It definitely was a day that changed my life. As a result of eight knee surgeries over 15 years I spent about eight years on crutches.

Crutches probably saved my life, because who knows what trouble I would have gotten into with two legs, no cast, and no crutches. I wasn't the dream patient. In fact, I once cut a cast off while my parents went on a cruise. The replacement cast I made was so thick it broke the doctor's saw. Another time I got caught climbing out my bedroom window in the dead of night. My boyfriend was holding my cast and crutches on the deck as I worked my way out the window. When my mom turned on the bedroom light he dropped everything and ran, leaving me straddling the hard window sill, one leg in and one casted leg out.

The dumbest thing I did was riding on the handlebars of a bicycle while my sister Susie pedaled, and her friend Donna was on the seat. We crashed, but I managed to leap gracefully off the falling bike and land on my good leg, balanced on my crutches, unscathed. Susie and Donna were not so lucky. When my mom asked how I got to the crash so fast I displayed my crutch running skills. You can imagine my shock when 50 years later she suddenly said, "You were on the handlebars weren't you?"

"Are you gonna ground me?" I had to ask.

Between random acts of foolishness, I did something that really influenced my life choices forever. One summer while all the other kids raged around the neighborhood, I read the complete set of LANDS AND PEOPLES ENCYCLOPEDIA. I read about the "Fuzzy Wuzzies" of Ethiopia – which goes to show how long ago this was. (They are now called by their correct name, Afar.) I read of lemurs in Madagascar and the temples of Thailand, the King of Swaziland and the Inca Trail in Peru. And, I've seen all of them, including meeting King Mswati III twice after he wrote the foreward to a kids' book I wrote about conservation in Swaziland.

But, back in the '60s, while in high school, when I slapped shut Volume XYZ of LANDS AND PEOPLES, I knew I would grow up to be a traveling fool and a writer. And that's exactly what I am.

I left the states in 1973 as a Peace Corps Volunteer going to Central America. I knew that I was going for more than two years, but I didn't know how. Just knew it would happen. Joe and I met in Peace Corps training in Puerto Rico. It didn't take long to realize how much we shared – especially the plan to see the world. He was assigned to Peru and I was assigned to Honduras, so I went to Tegucigalpa and he headed to Lima. Seven months later he transferred to Honduras. When I had the chance to move to the Bay Islands and said Joe and I should go together, the Peace Corps said, "Only if you're married." So, we decided to get married for one year — 44 years ago.

From 1973 through 2001, we spent 28 years in Africa, Latin America, Asia, the Caribbean, in fact on all seven continents. After five years as volunteers (1973 – '78) in three countries (Honduras/Peru, Kenya and the

Seychelles), we took our $18,000 Peace Corps readjustment allowance and headed to Ushuaia, Argentina, the southernmost town in the world. We traveled for three and a half years, with the only constraint being that we had to be in southern South America during their summer. We were open to all possibilities, and there were some amazing ones along the way that couldn't be planned or anticipated.

Eventually the trip took us from the Seychelles in the Indian Ocean back to Africa and 1,000 miles on a paddle-wheeled steamer down the Nile through Sudan. We spent seven months on a yacht in the Caribbean then headed to Venezuela. From there we started a two-year trip through South America that included five months on an uninhabited island in the Galapagos tagging turtles for the Darwin Research Station. When that rare opportunity was finished, we hit the road again, taking only public transport or hitchhiking from Ecuador to southern Chile, where we caught a ride with the Chilean Navy to Antarctica!

We traveled on the Piloto Pardo, an 81-meter icebreaker. My first step on the frozen continent came from a helicopter that was on the ship. During our three-and-a-half-week trip I hugged a penguin, drove the icebreaker to win a bottle of whiskey, and climbed up to the crow's nest 81 meters high. And, I danced the night away drinking Scotch on the rocks (broken from passing icebergs) with the officers. While I was dancing, Joe would go to bed. The officers on the ship started calling him *Poca Pila* – Low Battery. That was until we were caught in the shower together... Once we returned to Chile, it took another nine months to wander our way back up from Tierra Del Fuego to Ecuador. In Quito we had to admit that the funds were finally finished when we had only $18 left.

My in-laws provided tickets to New York, thinking we were finally ready to settle down, but how wrong they were. Within 10 days Joe had a job with CARE, the relief and development non-governmental organization, and we were on our way to Sierra Leone, and so began my life as an Ikut Swami.

To date, I have been to 110 countries and learned seven languages along the way. (I'd say there are only two and a half that I still speak.) And everywhere we went and lived I had the privilege of meeting, knowing, helping, laughing and working with local women. And we always had some type of connection as women, no matter how different our lives, skin colors, and education were.

The first time I heard the words Ikut Swami I was not a happy camper. We had just arrived in Lombok, Indonesia, and Joe's secretary, Winarte, had taken my passport for a visa. She brought it to the house and we were looking at it together. Proudly she pointed out the Ikut Swami phrase. "That is your occupation," she told me.

"Does it say writer/photographer?" I asked seriously, for that was what I planned to be.

"Oh no, it's better. It says Follows the Husband!"

The silence that followed was extremely heavy, finally broken by my shrieking voice when I said, "I don't think so."

Huffily, I asked her, "Do you think that's good?"

"Yes, very good. It's what a wife does."

"Take it back," I said. "They can put None or Nun for all I care, but Ikut Swami must go."

She looked at me with sadness and said, "So sorry, but it cannot be changed." Her expression left no doubt that I was the craziest *orang puti* — white person — she had ever met.

Obviously, the visa title was a done deal, and I knew I'd have to suck it up. I'm not sure exactly how many months it was before I started to calm down about it. And then after accepting it, I found myself astounded that I was even beginning to like it! When I thought about my life up until then, it was mainly true. Not in Peace Corps, but when we traveled for those three and a half years. Organized Joe always knew what bus to catch, road to stand on, and cheap hotel to check out for the night, which allowed me to be Cruiseamatic Cristina. The freedom it gave me was astounding.

Upon reflection, I realize that following Joe to Sierra Leone let me re-invent myself for my first re-incarnation. I began writing for kids for the first time in magazines like HIGHLIGHTS for CHILDREN and STEPPING STONES. My specialty was cross-cultural articles about kids in other countries, giving my readers trips to other worlds long before they had a passport. It was great and the beginning of a writing career that has produced five picture books, three Young Adult novels and three non-fiction books.

When we moved from Makeni, Sierra Leone, to Indonesia and the island of Lombok, the first island east of Bali, I knew I was going to try something different. There I got to be an undercover spy for The Star Report, which rated hotels around the world. That was a sweet job. I stayed in fancy hotels and wrote reviews. That led to writing the in-house magazine for the Sari Pacific, a 5-star hotel in Jakarta.

My first book, a coffee table book, LOMBOK – JUST BEYOND BALI, was published while we were there. My photography and text research took me to the remotest parts of Lombok, always escorted by Pulu, a young man from the tourism department. Traveling in Lombok meant visits to isolated villages, because that's all there was. My sudden arrival met with mixed reactions — mainly negative. Most kids had never seen an *orang puti* before and weren't happy. Panicked kids fled screaming, which led to frosty receptions and dangerous situations which meant we left quickly. And I got to all these places because I was an Ikut Swami.

The second time in Honduras, which followed Lombok, I wrote educational materials for a large agricultural NGO, and wrote my first YA novel, which is set in Sierra Leone, NO CONDITION IS PERMANENT. Ah, yes, free to pick what to pursue because I was an Ikut Swami.

Eventually, I would be a lot of things. In Niger, I did program evaluations for groups like Christian Children's

Fund. While we were there I wrote my first picture book, ONE NIGHT – A STORY FROM THE DESERT. That was followed by my second picture book set in West Africa, KONTE CHAMELEON – FINE, FINE, FINE!

After Niger, we took a seven-month trip to the South Pacific to renew our travel skills, then headed to Mozambique where Joe would be the Country Director for CARE. In true Ikut Swami style, I sat back and watched before deciding what to do. I discovered Swaziland, right next door, to be a great relief hatch from life in war-torn Mozambique.

Life in Mozambique was extremely challenging. Civil war raged for our first year, and so all travel outside of Maputo was in small airplanes, often single-engine. We had to fly high enough to stay out of rifle range, and land low and fast to avoid being shot. Swaziland was a great discovery, and soon I was visiting its wildlife parks as often as possible. I eventually wrote and photographed a non-fiction book for kids called ALL THE KING'S ANIMALS – THE REINTRODUCTION OF ENDANGERED SPECIES TO SWAZILAND. That's what an Ikut Swami can do. I also wrote JUBELA, my third picture book. It's a true story about a baby rhino adopted by an old matriarch

11

rhino when his mother was killed by poachers.

Sudan was next, and it was definitely one of the more challenging places we lived. We had been there in 1978 as wanderers and traveled the entire length of the Nile in Sudan from Juba in the far south, to Wadi Halfa on the Egyptian border, in a style of travel that I certainly won't ever do again. In 1978, Sudan was a land of proud and happy people, and nearly everyone we met felt sorry for us that we didn't live there. The Sudan we encountered 20 years later was war-torn and divided. Sharia Law ruled the land, and Khartoum was a much more somber spot.

Secret police lurked in front of our house, and scoring a beer was a real logistical event. While there, I was a full-time writer of picture books and travel articles. And every few months, I'd host an international women's potluck dinner and dancing party. Women from all over the world, including a few fearless Sudanese women, dressed in their very finest gowns and head ties (and me in my boring Western pants and tops) came with a dish to share after a good hour's worth of dancing. Dining was followed by a few more dances, and what had started at 5:00 was over by 8:00. I loved those nights, and they carried on to Ethiopia and Mali.

I guess you could say that as an Ikut Swami in Sudan I was an author and a women's party planner. It's also where I wrote MY GREAT-GRANDMOTHER'S GOURD, my fourth picture book, which is set in Sudan.

Ethiopia followed and was the most exciting and professionally rewarding of all. Teaching a writers' workshop for the British Council set me on a path I never could have imagined. I met Rahel Mekuria, and together we became a force to be reckoned with. Other dynamic Ethiopian women joined us in our endeavors, and together we founded a bi-lingual magazine called Women to Women or *Seytoch le Seytoch* in Amharic, which was years ahead of its time. The magazine was published by the British Council and distributed for free all over the country.

It was written by Ethiopian women for Ethiopian women, in English and Amharic. I was the English Editor, Rahel was the Editor-in-Chief, Mulu Mabeta was the Amharic Editor and Shitaye Astawes was the feature writer for articles about disabled women, and editor for the section. We tackled everything from health issues to women's rights to education and a debate page. We celebrated professional women and women helping women to help themselves. We rocked! The magazine was published twice a year for four years. But that wasn't all we accomplished.

I met Shitaye through Rahel. I had told Rahel one day that I had some crutches to give away (yes, another knee operation) and asked if she knew a woman who needed them. Rahel went to her good friend Shitaye, and when she told her about me giving away a pair of crutches she asked to meet me. It wasn't the reaction I expected at all. All four feet, three inches of Shitaye was full of indignation. In a matter of moments, she said, "You either give a lot or give nothing. One women with good crutches will be robbed for them – so either do a lot or do nothing."

"So, I'll do a lot," I said.

Rahel clapped and said, "That we will!" and Women on Wheels was born. With the help of my sister, Dianne Warren, WOW eventually got 3,020 women off the ground, but that's a whole different story. And all of this happened because I was an Ikut Swami, free to decide what to do wherever we were. FREE!

Mali was our last CARE post and international stop. While there I wrote my second and favorite YA novel, OUR SECRET, SIRI AANG, set in Kenya. I also taught writing workshops to kids and adults and did a little more consultation work as a program evaluator for small international NGOs. I began writing for in-flight magazines on Kenya Airways and Ethiopian Airlines. And, we traveled to Timbuktu four times, the setting of my last YA novel. Life as an Ikut Swami was still treating me well.

From the Sahara, we moved to the sea. St. John, to be exact, in the U.S. Virgin Islands. Joe had left CARE after 20 years for a job as the president of a small NGO called Friends of Virgin Islands National Park. Ikut Swami is still my style, and here I have taught writing workshops, from Let's Make a Picture Book for kids to a memoir writing class called Senior Moments for adults; been the Resident Author in the local elementary school; traveled the world as a visiting author; written for travel magazines; and finished my third YA novel, TROUBLE IN TIMBUKTU.

I have also written my last picture book, THE BEST BEEKEEPER OF LALIBELA, set in Ethiopia and my third non-fiction book called HOPE IS HERE, set in the Arctic Circle and St. Croix. It is my first book not set in Africa, and my sixth award-winning title.

But best of all, I've been able to continue trying to make a difference. If I don't have a project going I feel rotten, and so over the years here I've been taking and making the opportunities to raise money for causes I care about. I've found that most people, given the chance to help, will gladly do so. St. John is amazing in that sense because over the years the community has helped me raise more than $40,000 for different projects.

In 2001, local school kids here raised $5,000 for a water system in a Maasai village in Kenya. We had bake sales, collected and saved change for our Every Penny Counts bucket, and finished with a hug-a-thon where kids ran around a course manned by me and two friends. Each kid ran for three minutes, stopping to hug us as many times as possible, and then collecting a dollar a hug from sponsors. It was great! Then the community, through the St. John Rotary, matched our $5,000 bringing our total to $10,000.

Over three years I have organized and hosted an evening event to raise money for the Vhutshilo Mountain School (VMS) in Venda, South Africa. In three different nights over those years a small group of generous St. John residents gathered for an evening of magic — literally. My good friend, world-class magician Lisa Menna, (www.causetowonder.org) dazzled everyone at the first event and helped me find magicians for the next two years. Over those three nights we raised more than $30,000.00 for

VMS. The school works with pre-school kids and orphans that are HIV positive or have AIDS.

And through our 16 years here I have spent a lot of time on some beautiful beaches, snorkeled, dived and enjoyed Mother Nature. And now I'm a memoir writer! That's what an Ikut Swami can do!

I won't lie — I really miss our international life. The total unpredictability of what could happen any given day. The opportunity to be submerged in another culture. The chance to make friends with women around the world. Even though some of these encounters were very brief, they are still with me. The instant bond that usually formed was heart-warming and fun. And an honor for me. I have danced, worked, shared and laughed with women everywhere. I've had a chance to make a difference which makes me very happy.

TALES OF AN IKUT SWAMI is a collection of my experiences with women in the Developing World. Each country was a new adventure and a new challenge and being an Ikut Swami gave me the freedom to experience whatever opportunities came my way. Some of the stories are based on people that I knew for more than a year, and others lasted weeks, months, and in one case, an afternoon.

But each was recorded in a notebook or journal, which preserved details I definitely would have forgotten by now. One is a portion of an article I wrote for the early Ms. Magazine, but all the rest are recorded treasured memories. It would be great if these stories trigger a walk down Memory Lane for all that read the book, thinking about amazing women they have met. And it lets us know that some way, big or small, we can all make a difference.

I used to have a motto — ANY TRIP — ANYWHERE — ANY TIME! Now, I'm sorry to say, I've added BUT IT BETTER BE BUSINESS CLASS! I am so thankful that we wandered when the world was a safer place, and I was a more patient traveler. For I know without a doubt that I couldn't do today what we did then. I'm so thankful I met all these women from Mali to Bali, Zanzibar to Addis Ababa, South Pacific to Sudan to South Africa. I hope you enjoy meeting them, too.

Writing this intro has made me appreciate my great life as an Ikut Swami. Thank you, Joe, for giving me the freedom to wait, watch and choose. And thanks to all the generous people who have enabled me to keep making a difference. In my opinion — it doesn't get better than that for a full-time Ikut Swami!

THE FRIGHTENED BRIDE
Lamu, Kenya
1976

Lamu is a beautiful island off the east coast of Kenya in the Indian Ocean. Its inhabitants and spirit convey a trip of time and distance — to ages past and places far. A half-hour sail on a dhow during the rise of a full moon is really the only way to arrive. Short, white buildings line the winding alleys that serve as the main thoroughfares through the village. Intricately carved, heavy wooden doors shut out the few foreigners who wandered the narrow passageways. Women draped in the traditional *bui-buis*, long, black gowns revealing only dark eyes lined with henna, rush down the winding paths, living shadows on the run.

Black Africa, only miles away, was not evident in this Arab enclave.

Lamu was first settled by disgruntled religious outcasts from Persia and Arabia as far back as the seventh century. Unlike the missionaries and white farmers who would come to East Africa several centuries later, the Muslims created a strong Arab/Islam following through marriage with the coastal Africans. The combination produced a people and *lingua franca* called Swahili.

19

Not much has changed in the ensuing centuries. Arab dhows still ply the coast with their distinctive slanted sails, and only one car drove slowly through the crowded streets. This lonely vehicle belonged to the obviously out-of-place Kikuyu police commissioner and his crew, clear reminders for the people who often forget that they are Kenyans and not citizens of an independent Arab state. The island has a turbulent history of wars and feuds. It was also a famous port for slave ships terrorizing the East African coast.

We arrived in time to attend a large wedding that was underway. The wedding was not confined in a house or mosque, but happening in the streets, with the entire community involved. Strangers were welcome. We fell in behind a long procession of chanting women, all clad in black. They wove through the congested streets like a long, slumberous snake, moving to the eerie sound of clacking sticks that were rhythmically struck by the lines of dancing, weaving women.

The procession ended outside an enclosed area, reserved for women only. I waved goodbye to Joe as a newfound friend swept me into the enclosure with her brigade of black-clad women.

The scene that awaited me was a shock. All those shy,

overly clad women were shedding their *bui-buis* as fast as kids dropping their pants to swim, then strutting their stuff with an enthusiasm I never expected. Minus the black veils and gowns was a showcase array of low-cut cocktail dresses, flashy gold necklaces, and intricate high-rise hairdos, reminiscent of June Cleaver on a big night out. At least half of the attending women were removing their restrictive clothing, demonstrating the wealth and beauty that normally only their husbands witness.

And there I was, in baggy pants and a T-shirt in a sea of strutting women. One grabbed my hand and led me to her friends. In a matter of seconds three women were braiding my hair as I stood there like a hippy in the headlights. Then another woman ran her hands down the front of my T-shirt, I assume to get the wrinkles out. The finishing touch was a beautiful frangipani flower attached to each of the three braids. I'd never had an instant makeover before, and I actually enjoyed it. I'd also never worn three braids at once, so I was stylin'! A few shoulder pats and hand tugs assured me that I was party-ready.

Together we wove our way toward the front of the crowd. Central to the celebrations was a throne that resembled a '57 Chevy convertible awaiting its homecoming queen. It was a shiny red vinyl couch on a raised platform, decorated with pink plastic flowers, Indian mats, bright pink pillows and flashing Christmas lights.

The throne was vacant, but seated next to it in an obvious place of honor, was a stern-faced woman. Neither the general buzz of conversation nor the charged atmosphere fazed her in her serious pose. Finally, the bride arrived. She couldn't have been more than 14 and looked far from an elated bride.

She entered wearing a *bui-bui*, which was carefully removed by anxious attendants, revealing a shocking pink gown that clashed horribly with her stoplight red throne. A white veil covered her head, and long white gloves climbed to her elbows. The big rings adorning her covered fingers reflected the flashing Christmas lights around her head, and in the land of fresh orchids and jasmine, she clutched a bouquet of plastic flowers. Installed on her throne, she looked entranced and terrified. At no time did she look directly at any of her numerous well-wishers. Instead, she maintained a motionless pose with eyes downcast and her face severely solemn.

Slowly, women began to mount the dais and pin shillings to her dress. As the count and amount increased, another woman began unpinning the money and attaching it to the pink pillows.

Meanwhile, two other women were passing through the crowd with smoking jasmine incense burners. Women still attired in their *bui-buis* quickly enclosed the burners inside their robes until smoke flowed out the top like so many restless volcanoes. The thick rich smell, nearly as dense as the smoke, permeated the air. At least six of my new friends flicked smoke my way with their practiced hands. Bounteous food trays followed, stacked high with totally unidentifiable food objects.

The atmosphere of gaiety was suddenly struck silent as a white man entered the enclosure with a camera. He moved up to the dais to photograph the bride and her crew. With rigid posture and serious faces, the friends and relatives stood in groups of two with the bride. I could only hope that the expressions of the wedding party were not reflections of the life the bride was about to begin. With the arrival of the photographer, all the women were forced to replace their *bui-buis* and resume the serious demeanor ascribed to Arab women.

A commotion outside the enclosure heralded the arrival of the groom and his friends and relatives. Another new friend grabbed my hand and led me to the entrance. Her *bui-bui* covered her from head to toe, leaving only her shining eyes exposed.

She looked out into the street and surprised me when she said, "You are lucky. You are a woman, so you came inside. Your husband awaits you."

"You speak English?" I blurted out.

"Oh yes, but I didn't want to disturb you inside. We loved that you danced and ate and celebrated with us. My friends have asked me to tell you this. And to thank you for joining us."

Without another word, she steered me to Joe, outside the enclosure, who was temporarily dazzled by my new look. As fast as my English-speaking friend disappeared, we were surrounded by a procession of young, singing boys. They were followed by a group of serious old men, who were followed by the groom, sheltered beneath an umbrella carried by a wizened old man on a rainless, star-studded night. The groom looked extremely handsome in his long-brocaded robe, Arab turban, and dangling sword. His face was older than the bride's, but as solemn as the sad young girl's waiting inside the enclosure. Following the groom were two drummers and 50 more black-clad women, swaying to the rhythm of the stick dance, singing softly. We waited to see if the groom would join his bride inside the enclosure, but he didn't.

Instead, there was a sudden flow of bui-buis from the enclosed area, as the women began to filter out. Properly attired for the public view, plunging necklines, flashy jewels and fancy hairdos were hidden from sight. The groom entered a house directly opposite the enclosure, and soon after, his reluctant bride whooshed across the alley in her bui-bui to meet her solemn handsome groom for the very first time.

A SEA OF NIPPLES
Nile Steamer, Sudan
1978

One thing is certain — it was the trip of a lifetime — meaning it will NEVER be repeated. One thousand miles on the Nile steamer, from Juba in southern Sudan to Kosti in the north. This lifetime trip tested all of my traveler's skills and then some. Nothing was easy, in fact everything was a challenge, from peeing to sleeping to eating to bathing.

Cooking took on new dimensions of difficulty. Our food supply consisted of canned goods, things like Chef Boyardee Spaghetti, Bully Beef, and equally unappetizing mini-wieners. To round off the menu, we also had rice and a few potatoes. We were thankful for the canned goods, but I was self-conscious about them. They seemed to accentuate the gap between us and all the other boat passengers. One small area on the back of a front barge was filled with women. From sunup to sundown they worked the charcoal burners for their families. It was the women's space and social center.

This was also my cooking space. My appearance on the scene always livened things up, for I was definitely like a

UFO landing. I was never sure which attracted more attention, my presence, or the weird slippery things I was forever dumping out of tinned cans.

The women were great. My attempts to ignite dry charcoal with a truly inexperienced hand provided endless entertainment. They all giggled at the white apparition. Before long, one woman would lift white-hot coals, barehanded, from her burner and set them in mine. Others would quickly follow suit, and soon I would have blazing heat rising from my coal pot.

The second act consisted of producing some canned delicacy for that day's meal. Slimy spaghetti and stubby mini-wieners always got a good laugh. I would offer tastes around, but there were never any takers.

Cleaning up after cooking involved squatting on the edge of the barge dipping pots and plates into the rushing river for a cursory cleansing. On the second day, Joe's cleaning activities on the barge where we slept coincided with a rather serious bump against the bank. My plate promptly floated away, so I ate out of our Frisbee for the rest of the trip, which eventually took us all the way to Antarctica and back.

All of my cooking partners were Nuer women. Nuers,

like Dinkas and Shilluks, are cattle people of the south. That is about the only similarity amongst the tribes, for each bares a specific pattern of scarification that identifies their tribe immediately. The scars serve as beautification, as well as protection against illness. The faces of my Nuer cooking companions were decorated with sets of three-inch carved crevices. Thick grooves had been cut into their foreheads in a pattern of three deeply etched horizontal lines. I winced at the thought of the pain involved in creating these adornments. They say that the skull of a Nuer is easily identified by the indentations left on the skull bone.

My cooking buddies, in traditional Nuer style, all wore matted cow dung on their hair. The combination of black, scarred skin and white, stiff hair was striking. I felt like their photo negative with my dark hair and white skin. We were not inhibited by our inability to chat. I wore a conga or sarong, and one day it slipped open, making my right knee visible. Running around the curve of my kneecap and down the front of my shin is a scar from six knee operations. One woman intently traced the path of my scar on my leg, then traced it on my face. Slowly she dragged her finger around the rim of my left eye socket, then straight down my cheek. A perfect replica of the scythe-shaped scar on my leg.

I am sure she was asking, "Why do you hide this righteous scar under your long skirt? Why don't you wear such a beauty on your face?"

The days casually evolved into a loose schedule. Breakfast was a can of peaches or pears. The empty cans became our toilet facilities, requiring a deadeye aim from an eyeless area. After the bathroom call, we would set forth to wander amongst our friendly fellow passengers. Given the degree of difficulty, cooking was done only once a day by me. This left us with a lot of free time.

One day we decided to visit the captain, a large, bronze-colored man, the final product of a merging of the north and south, Arab and Black Sudan. The captain greeted us cordially. Dressed in a loose flowing robe that resembled a hospital gown, he continually stroked his bald head. He spoke a very halting English from his captain's chair. Musa Kamal had been working on the river for 41 years and had been skipper of the steamer for 16 years.

"There's a 25-year apprenticeship," he told us. "You must learn all the sandbars and currents in all the seasons, and that takes time."

The style of steering was unique and quickly clarified the reason for the ricocheting progress. The captain sat off to one side, giving instructions to two crew members who manned a very large steering wheel.

"Right, right, no left, left, right, right," he shouted in Arabic. Wrestling with the 6-foot wheel, the two helmsmen frantically guided us into the bank. Sitting in his chair, the captain pulled back on the throttle, sending the paddle wheel into reverse to wrench us from the bank, and line up for the next crash.

The steamer we were traveling on had been built in 1954 and appeared to be suffering from severe neglect. (This same steamer sank three years later, with a death toll of more than 1,000 people.) There were broken handrails and peeling paint everywhere. The cables were frayed and broke with an alarming frequency.

On day three, while I stood on a back barge and Joe on one in the front row, the cable connecting our two barges snapped.

Joe's barge was swept forward by the current and he yelled, "See you in Kosti. I have the passports."

"That's OK," I shouted back. "I have the money."

It took six hours to maneuver and refasten the barges,

a quick repair compared to some of the other breakdowns. Sitting on the rooftop gave us a great vantage point for bird, crocodile, and hippo watching. It also gave us the chance to smoke an occasional joint and breathe some fresh air.

The boat had been loaded with dried fish in Bor. Hanging between half consumed stocks of bananas, the fish sent out an odor that competed with the local tobacco for pungency power. The air was heavier each day with the accumulation of rotten food, feces, tobacco, and dried fish.

Sitting up high provided a perfect view of our fellow passengers. Although I was cooking in the Nuer kitchen, there were hundreds of Dinkas and Shilluks on board, too. The Dinka stood out as everyone was wearing some sort of jewelry, be it thick ivory biceps bracelets or ivory rings with 6-inch prongs. Walking amidst these 7-foot-tall people was like entering an ebony forest. I often felt suspended in a sea of nipples, standing far below shoulder height.

The hairdo of the Dinka women was uniformly repeated, and beautiful. Each woman had a head full of tightly plaited braids. Incorporated into each braid was a piece of black yarn to give it the length that hadn't come naturally. My long dark hair was often stroked appreciatively, with an occasional tug thrown in to see if it would come loose.

There is no such thing as a fat Dinka. They are long and lean. Dedicated semi-nomadic cattle people, curiously they also make very good townspeople. Most civil service positions in the south were filled by Dinkas. No matter how high a Dinka rises in the civil service, he is still considered a regular person when he returns to his village. He'll be the butt of jokes from his childhood friends, just to refresh his memory of who he is and where he comes from. When he marries, he must still provide up to 50 cattle as a bride price and pursue his bride in the traditional manner.

One day, while making a routine leap from one moving barge to the next, I slipped in something too rude to mention. Reaching desperately for support, someone gently grabbed my hand. Slowly standing upright, I gazed into the face of a Shilluk woman, just a breath away. Bumpy scars just above her eyebrows looked as though she had planted a string of pearls below the skin's surface at the base of her forehead. Flashing her Colgate smile we walked hand-in-hand to our tiny cabin, then she wandered on.

The Shilluks, like the Dinkas and Nuers, originated from the Nilote nomads who wandered south from Egypt in ages past. They also are fiercely attached to their cattle. Settled on the fertile banks of the Nile north of Malakal, they are well-known throughout the Sudan as successful cattle breeders, fishermen and farmers.

The Shilluk are like the bird kingdom because the males are resplendent in their personal appearance, and the women are more subdued. Each Shilluk warrior wore a wig of animal hair that was knotted into their own hair. The wigs are a sign of affluence as they grow with periodic updates. Ostrich feathers also adorn the unique shapes and sizes of hairpieces. These often bizarre, but definitely arresting wigs are bordered by the string of scars that adorn all Shilluks across the base of the forehead — the string of submerged pearls. Ouch. Shilluk means "scar" in Arabic.

One day I saw the rare sight of three women, each from a different tribe, sitting together. They had no common language but were enjoying each other's company. The Shilluk woman patted the Nuer's lady's cow-dung do, while the Nuer woman ran her hand along the Dinka woman's arm, like she was reading Braille as she skimmed across the raised bumps of the decorative scars. The Dinka woman counted the buried pearls on the Shilluk woman's forehead. It was a beautiful sight that just reinforced my feelings that if women ran the world it would be a much safer place. There was admiration instead of jealousy. Friendliness instead of competition.

On the final day as our battered barge conglomeration floated into Kosti, Joe and I moved to the front of our barge for a quick exit. Before we could leave a Nuer woman grabbed my hand. She was a fellow cook and she pointed at her friends. Together they ululated and waved, and I waved back. The trip that had been a challenge for me was a mini-vacation for them. For six days they didn't have to search for firewood or carry water on their heads. They had six days to lounge, laugh, and relax. Now they were ready to resume their busy lives. And I was ready for a bath!

SUKA HATI
Lombok, Indonesia
1984

In 1983, Joe and I learned that we were being transferred to Indonesia. Two years in Makeni, Sierra Leone, had really worn me out. I'd had hepatitis, diagnosed by two veterinarians. One day, our dog Budley died in my lap after being bitten by a green mamba. Looking away from his pain I saw the tennis clubhouse — a little shanty with six clothes hooks on the wall — burning down. It was a bad day, one of many in Makeni. The sudden news of moving to Lombok, Indonesia, was wonderful news.

Sierra Leone was a challenging place in 1981-'83. We lived in a slanted house that backed up onto pure bush. I got a ricocheted lightning strike in bed one night. The next morning a green mamba was wrapped around the inside kitchen door handle. The snake was 10 feet from where I had spent the remainder of the night on a mattress on the floor. I freaked out, screaming, "You win Makeni."

I bailed on Joe three weeks early. The one and only time I left a country first.

The first thing I did when I got to the States was buy an Indonesian dictionary, to figure out a title for my journals I kept so diligently back then. I had already completed a five-set series of embossed journals, called variations of Rolling Stoned. Then there were two volumes of Bo Bound, the name of the journals for Sierra Leone. When we got to Freetown the CARE staff told us, "Sorry. Not Bo, but a place called Makeni."

Maybe having the wrong title set the tone for life in Sierra Leone, which was a never-ending run of challenges. All I knew is that I didn't want to choose the wrong title again in our move to Indonesia. To set the right vibe I put together two words from my dictionary, Suka Hati — I Am Content. Or so I thought.

One afternoon, my Balinese friend, Winarte, came by our house in Lombok. She was also Joe's secretary and my go-to person. She knew I was working on my first book, a photo book called LOMBOK – JUST BEYOND BALI. She was all excited as she came in the door, asking if I wanted to go to the Balinese palace in Ampenam and take some photos for my book. I was writing in my journal when she walked in. I closed the book as she sat down, and her face went from happy and excited to stunned.

Her discomfort was obvious. I could see her flush beneath her beautiful brown skin. I knew that an

Indonesian will go a long way to avoid causing someone to lose face. Her discomfort could only mean one thing; we were clearly on the brink of one of those moments.

Reaching her graceful hand out she tapped my journal. "I was just wondering about your title, Suka Hati…"

"I picked it," I bragged. "It means "I Am Content." Her look confirmed I had picked another wrong title for my journal. Dropping her eyes to spare me any embarrassment Winarte said, "No. It means 'I Love Liver.'"

We both burst out laughing, for I was a total vegetarian at the time. Once we could talk again she suggested I get my camera and we head to the palace. Little did we know as we left the house that our belly laugh would soon be replaced by total shame, embarrassment and tears.

The drive across Mataram was as hectic as ever. Winarte drove slowly as she dodged *cidomos*, the horse carts that filled the roads. There was also an endless stream of pedestrians, like the movies had just let out. Motorcycles carrying families of five or more, dodged in and out of the traffic. Chaos reigned, but our mood was buoyant as we finally reached the Mayura Water Palace, built in 1744 as part of the Balinese royal court in Lombok.

We pulled up to a dramatic stone archway that had a thick blue wooden door. The arch stood on the edge of a large man-made lake. Winarte had a beautiful purple potted orchid in one hand — a gift for the prince who was living there. She knocked on the ornate wooden door, and it was opened immediately. Winarte looked at me and said, "They are expecting us."

An older woman greeted us, and we stepped into an enchanted place. The noise and chaos of town diminished with each step we took into the palace grounds. On a giant lake sat a beautiful building, called a floating pavilion, that sat at the far end of the walkway on the lake.

As usual, I felt like the Jolly Green Giant. Winarte walked in front of me, all of five feet tall. Our escort even smaller, walked behind me. Both women, small and fragile, were nearly a foot shorter than me. I won't even make a weight comparison.

Half-way to our destination we passed a small building set off a short distance to the side of the walkway. I asked Winarte if it was a detached kitchen. Without stopping she said, "Oh no, it's for women on their periods. They are not allowed in the main house during that time."

I stopped dead in my tracks, and the little lady behind

crashed into me. "Winarte, I'm on my period. We have to come back another time."

She thought a moment then said, "No, it is alright because you are a foreigner. It's not the same thing."

"Are you sure?" I asked.

"One hundred percent," she replied.

A young man awaited us in the palace. He wasn't "officially" a king, but he had descended from kings of the Balinese Karangasem Dynasty. He was in his 30s and was the great-great-great-grandson of the first Balinese king on Lombok. He looked like every Balinese man — short thick black hair, a sarong and shirt. No footmen or crown. He offered us tea, and as we waited he took me around the room, pointing out various artworks on the walls, statues and woven cloths.

"This was the Palace of Justice," he told me proudly.

He graciously let me take photos of the various objects. As we sat for tea, I complimented him on all of his fine treasures. When he said I hadn't seen the best item yet, I prayed he meant it was still to be revealed.

"It is a hat," he told us proudly. "It is full of powers that helped my ancestors rule."

I blurted out, "I have a hat collection — from 31

countries. I would love to see your power hat if at all possible."

It didn't take much convincing. As he left the room Winarte touched the back of my hand and said, "He likes you."

From that moment, I decided he really was a king. He returned about five minutes later, carrying a beautiful burnished box. The hat box had four little clasps, each with a small lock. He unlocked them, one by one, then lifted the top slat off and the four sides fell outward. It was very dramatic.

There sat the power hat. It looked like a gladiator's helmet, narrow on the top with a flared brim. Running around the brim was a magnificent collection of precious stones and pearls. The sun shining in at the perfect angle spotlighted the green topaz, red rubies, dazzling diamonds and a huge iridescent pearl. There were stones I'd never seen before of all shapes and sizes. We each gazed at it in silence, absorbing its beauty and power.

"Amazing," I whispered. I lifted my camera and asked, "May I take one photo?"

"Oh no," he said, still gazing at the hat. "There are only two ways the hat can lose its power — if a picture is taken, or a menstruating woman looks at it."

I saw Winarte's eyes pop open wide as mine slammed shut. I turned my back to the hat before I opened them again. Winarte's face was more distressed then when she'd told me about "I Love Liver". Grabbing my hand, she told the king, "Thank you so much for this wonderful visit. I am sure it is one we shall never forget. But I must get back to my work."

The king asked, "You are not upset that I won't allow a photo, are you?"

Shaking my head and looking everywhere else, I said, "Not at all. I appreciate you telling me 'no.' We are just leaving suddenly because we have taken too much of your time already. And Winarte must get back to work."

I had never seen Winarte move so fast. We departed much quicker than we arrived. I looked her way as we got in the car. I had seen her flush at having to tell me about my journal title, but now we were both flaming red, filled with shame and an element of fear. We didn't say a word the whole way to my house. The chaos outside our car windows was mild compared to the chaos in our hearts and minds.

When she screeched to a halt in our driveway she said,

not looking at me, "Please go light many incense sticks. I must get home and make more offerings than I have made in my lifetime." Shaking her head slowly she said, "I have made a terrible mistake."

"We have," I said. A quick hug and she was gone.

I felt sick to my stomach, as did she. I was glad that I had told her right from the beginning about my period. I would have felt a gazillion times worse if I had made the call to go inside regardless of my "unclean" state. One thing I knew for sure, we both owned the terrible cultural gaffe.

That night the most intense thunder and lightning storm we had ever experienced pounded Mataram and Ampenam. With each shocking bolt of lightning I could see Winarte's face again from the afternoon — eyes popped open wide. The thunder sounded like our feet pounding out the door. Joe held me tight, for he knew about the power hat and the period.

The next morning, I went to visit Winarte. Her usual impeccable appearance was a little ragged looking. She also hadn't slept all night long. She dropped her bloodshot eyes in shame and said, "I am very sorry. It was all my fault. I do not know what made me think there is a difference between an *orang puti* woman — a foreigner — and us. We are all women with the same monthly challenge. I am sorry for thinking you are less."

I patted her shoulder and assured her, "I should have known better myself. For as you say, we are all women." Then I said, "Oh my God! Was that storm amazing or what? Do you think it could have been a…" and in that moment we both said, "cleansing?"

Winarte nodded her head and said, "I pray that the power of the storm restored the power of the hat. I pray, I pray."

She looked down at her lap, fixed something and then lifted an elegant watertight woven box holding a floating frangipani flower. She placed it on her desk and said, "This is our offering to say thank you for the storm."

We gazed silently at its beauty then I asked, "Do you think the hat is OK?"

"I will never know," she said, "for I shall never return to the palace unless invited. I guess if I am invited back it means the hat is fine, but who knows if or when that may happen."

"Have you been invited before?"

"Yes, many times. My father was a well-known priest."

Lifting her eyes from the offering she said, "It is the first time I am not saddened that he is no longer here. If I disgraced him there would be no recovering from that."

I leaned over and hugged her. "We have learned a great lesson," I told her. "I am sure we knew it before but now we know it for sure — all women are created equal. And if our prayers and shame last night brought on the storm then we also know that women are powerful. Please don't let this affect our friendship in a negative way. We have had a life lesson together."

Winarte hugged me back, and I could feel the tension easing from her body.

It was four months before she received an invitation to the palace. Four very long months. During that time, she was a subdued Winarte. On her visit, they explained that they had all been gone, visiting family and temples on Bali and Java. Her spirit soared when the hat was not mentioned, and her spark returned. She had finally forgiven herself. No news of the hat showed just how powerful it was — for it gave us both back our peace of mind.

THE PISTOL IN PARADISE
Niue, South Pacific
1991

I'd seen her all over town — looking like the busiest person in Niue. Her short black hair was sprinkled with grey. She was built like a fireplug but active like a smoldering volcano. She was always looking for straight answers and pushing for plans of action. It didn't take long for us to finally meet. Seeing the glint in her eye I knew that she was a real pistol, not just hot air.

Looking at me with her shining eyes, O'love "Veve" Jacobsen said, "I've created Merry Hell in this country since 1988."

That was when she was first elected to the House of Assembly in a bi-election. Since that time, she's proud to say, "I've stirred up a lot by challenging old systems, old governing styles, and best of all, old men."

Niue, not exactly a common household word, is a small, twice up-raised coral atoll in the South Pacific. I had chosen to visit there because, as I told Joe, "It's the shortest chapter in the South Pacific handbook."

Many things make it unique. Unlike other South Pacific island nations, it is a single island rather than a group. It

had a resident population of 2,200 people, while about
12,000 Niueans live in New Zealand. Its total land mass of
256 square kilometers takes about two hours to drive
around on a motor scooter, passing through shaded forest
areas, taro fields and jagged coral outcrops. It's also special
because it doesn't have one sand beach. Sitting high above
the water, the easiest way to go scuba diving was to wait for
high tide. You could jump from the one island dock into
the sea, and then climb a ladder out. It was a challenge.

In 1974, Niue became a self-governing nation in free
association with New Zealand. That "special relationship"
meant that New Zealand would continue to provide
administrative and economic assistance to maintain a viable
community. In 1988, it still had its original Premier, Sir
Robert Rex.

Speaking her mind Veve told me, "Men have balled
this place up, and now it's time for women to come in and
clean up the mess."

Her fellow islanders consider her a real fighter, not
afraid to tackle issues and problems that have gone
unchallenged for years.

She came into the public eye when she led a workers'
strike against management of Niue's only hotel. "It was an

interesting situation," she said, "because my husband was the manager. So, there we were, husband and wife on opposite sides of the table." That was her first brush with politics, and the community recognized her as a leader and have supported her actively since then.

Under the local system there is a representative from each village in the House Assembly. There are six additional seats, elected island-wide on the common roll. In April of 1990, she led the common roll of 21 candidates.

"I've told my colleagues I should be premier as the person who's won the most votes in Niue." It was obvious she wasn't joking.

"Sir Robert is over 80, and his days as premier are numbered. He's done some good things, but it's time for him to gracefully step down. But he won't. Others are doing his thinking for him. He's an old gun with new bullets that goes pssst instead of bang."

It was obvious she had her eye on the premiership.

"I'm the only level-headed one around in the turmoil. Right now, it's basically a lot of old men frightened by a new drake."

In her opinion, the caretakers of the millions of dollars of aid money from New Zealand need to be prudent and accountable.

"The previous and current governments have not been accountable."

She sights cultural elements as the reason for the unchallenged system. "Things like respect for elders and the unapproachable status of politicians are holding us back. Also, it's a very small place, and people fear being victimized or becoming unpopular by speaking out. If you rock the boat and fall out, you could end up with nothing."

Rocking the boat is just what she does best. In March of '91, the New Zealand government announced a cut of NZ $500,000 from a NZ 9.5 million-dollar budget.

"What is this government's solution? Let's cut 120 jobs from public service — Niue's largest employer. That's roughly one fourth of the employed population."

Shaking her head, she said, "The private sector can't support 120 jobless. New Zealand has told us since 1988 that the public service is too big."

Stretching out her arms she laughed as she said, "The body is too big for the dress. We have a Polynesian body trying to squeeze into a European dress."

It's no surprise that she had a plan already.

"I'd cut the work week to 36 hours, cutting off work

time rather than jobs. This gives individual departments a deadline for raising revenue and decreasing costs — so productivity being improved is what we really need. We don't need 120 newly unemployed."

Something that makes Niue unusual is that when, and if the cuts happen, women won't automatically be the first to go.

"We don't suffer from open sexual discrimination here. It is so quiet and subtle that you can't pick it up easily." In such a small place, everyone knows everyone. In 1994, the First Lady of Niue, Lady Rex, and Veve attended a conference in Roaratonga representing Niue. The UN conference was called "Elimination of All Forms of Discrimination Against Women." Each participating country presented papers.

Veve was proud to say, "We learned one thing — women in Niue have more freedom than most women in the Pacific. Lady Rex has been active in women's rights here. She's a much better politician than her husband, the premier. It's like I told her, you've got a silver platter and I have a pandamus mat!"

For whatever reason, Veve has not been elected premier, and it's not for lack of trying. She's run numerous times, but like she says, "Old men still hang on tight to the reins."

This doesn't mean she hasn't been busy. From 1993 to 1999 she has been the Minister of Environment, Education and Culture; the Minister of Ethnic Arts and Religion; Minister of Sports and Youth Affairs and, in 2008, the Minister of Health. She's currently running for premier in the 2017 so the activist is still in action.

When I asked her one day if she ever relaxes, she said, "I do just like you. We women work hard, and something tells me that you are also a fighter for women's rights. We all work in our way, but we all work toward the same thing. It's funny because I think we have more rights here than you do in America. And I can tell you that because you and I are women - women who listen."

Then she patted my shoulder and said, "Just remember, no vacation lasts forever!"

I'll never forget meeting her the first time at Jenna's Bakery. She was talking to me, serving customers, taking loaves of hot fresh bread from the oven and taking a call from the Minister of Human Services. And during it all she took a $20 bill from the cash register and put it into an elderly woman's bread bag.

The old lady's eyes lit as Veve said, "Not to worry sister. We all need a little help from time to time."

WE ARE THE SAME WOMAN
Zanzibar Island, Tanzania
1994

The end of Ramadan was on Tuesday. The moon finally appeared as slender as the sheerest almond sliver, but definitely visible, off the coast of Zanzibar. Wednesday was Eid, the feast day to celebrate the end of the year's month-long fasting period. The day was for killing goats and eating great quantities of food between prayer sessions. And for dressing up and meeting with friends and families or strolling the beaches that are usually the workday environment.

Wednesday was also the first day that not a woman was working on her seaweed *shamba* in the crystalline waters. Zanzibar is as beautiful as the name always conjured for me when I dreamt of walking the beaches of the island, as a kid far, far away in California. It was my ultimate destination at the age of 12. The island of my dreams. And it was no disappointment, 44 years later when we finally got there.

It's a dream blending of warm, tropical waters that range between lake calm and pounding surf and swaying palm trees lining long white sweeps of beach. Shell collecting along the high tide line can fill a calm morning.

Nearly each evening the gentle afternoon breezes rise to a rough whisper as the emerald afternoons drift into topaz evenings and fire opal sunsets. The people complete the picture.

For days, I had been watching and talking to women working in their seaweed *shambas* when the tide dropped. *Shamba* is Swahili for a small farm or vegetable plot, and until recently only referred to farms on land. Today, there is a thriving industry of small seaweed farms all along the east coast of Zanzibar.

I met Nyuziani one morning as she worked on her plot, — her hands, gnarled with age, and her skin wrinkled from a life in the African sun. But still her fingers worked nimbly with the seaweed stems and fishing line as she stood bent in half at the waist.

"I'm less than 100," she told me, even though I hadn't asked, "but my daughter is a grandmother, so you figure it out."

She was stretching her tired back as she looked at her skein of sticks placed in a distinct arrangement in the shallow waters left behind by the spring tides.

"It is much cooler to work in the water, but the glare is hurting my eyes. So, some days I spend in my land *shamba* where I grow tomatoes, papaya, and millet to sell, and some days here. I always come during spring tides, when the water is the lowest the longest."

Her Swahili was hypnotizing, for Zanzibar has the purest spoken Swahili in the world. My Swahili was doable. I could understand and be understood.

In 1992, a Filipino man came to the village at Uroa Beach and introduced the idea of producing seaweed for sale. The women jumped at the chance right away since they didn't need to buy land, weed or water the plots, or give up precious *shamba* space to a new, unknown crop. He brought with him the basic tools of the trade — wooden stakes 10 centimeters long and fishing line. The rest was already awaiting them in the sea.

In the tropics, seaweed thrives between the low-tide line and a depth of about 200 meters. This leaves a lot of planting space for the women in Zanzibar, for tidal drops are extreme. At low tide it's possible to walk in shallow water for nearly 300 meters off the beach. Most women plant within the first 100 meters of the shoreline making it easier to get the heavy, waterlogged sacks home.

To create a plot for a seaweed *shamba,* the women first lay out a grid pattern of sticks, stuck into the sand. The sticks stand upright, and a web of fishing line is tied from one stake to another, connecting all sticks vertically and horizontally in rows. Then, with infinite patience, they tie strands of seaweed along the connecting lines.

With the flow of the current these strands feed on the nutrients in the water and grow along the suspended lines. The sticks are situated so that the seaweed is always covered with water, regardless of how low the tide. There are 24 sticks in one plot, producing an average income of 40,000 Tanzanian shillings per plot per month. At 75 shillings per kilo of seaweed, that's a lot of seaweed produced on a monthly basis. Unfortunately for the women, the Filipino man only buys dried seaweed. One dried bag equals six wet bags.

Zuwena, a 45-year-old woman with four kids, basically prefers working on her seaweed *shamba* to working on land. The returns are so much greater from the sea and the work so much easier — if you discount the glare on her eyes.

"I make enough money to pay school fees, buy uniforms, and pens and books for my children," she says proudly. "It's not enough to really save money, but our life is better now. We eat and sell from our *shamba* on land. We get cash from our *shamba* in the sea."

The Filipino man comes once a week to buy the dried seaweed for export to the Far East. Throughout Asia, especially in Japan, seaweed is a commercially important food. People use it in soups and sauces and sometimes salads. The women of Zanzibar, who grow it, don't eat it.

The middleman has informed them that if it is not prepared correctly then it is poisonous. This is clearly a ruse to protect his supply, but it's probably not necessary. Nyuziana admits to having tried it once, but the heavy, salty taste made her feel "like I was chewing the sea. It's better to sell it and buy something to eat that tastes good."

Nyuziana, who has been working her plot for three years, is thinking of turning it over to her granddaughters, for her eyes are suffering. The incidence of cataracts has increased significantly since seaweed *shambas* began, and the theory, because most sufferers are women, is that it's a result of working in the sea.

During spring tides, the women spend up to four hours a day in their plots, sitting or bending very close to the reflective surface of the water that beams back the sun. During the rest of the moon's cycle they spend a maximum of one and a half hours a day in the glare. So, work that is less demanding physically, still takes its toll.

If Nyuziana does give up her seaweed *shamba*, she won't be out of work. There is a new cottage industry cropping up — the preparing and selling of sticks. Most sticks must be carved down to the correct size, while others can be collected from the beach. When surf or wind is really up, both sticks and seaweed are thrown ashore. Young girls and women of all ages can be seen scouring the beach, filling bags of seaweed from plants torn loose and collecting the dislodged sticks.

"I can collect things on the beach," Nyuziana says, "for I've done that my whole life. But by making sticks I can sit in the shade and still work all the day long." Twenty-five sticks, sharpened at one end and rubbed smooth, cost between 300 and 400 shillings. Combined with a small business of selling bags, Nyuziana can easily support her family without the wear and tear on her eyes.

"I can make as much as I did when I spent all those days in the water. And not hurt my eyes or break my back bending like a bent rod."

"How soon do you think you'll move into the shade?" I asked her.

"As soon as the school year ends. My granddaughters must go to school."

Slowly I took off my sunglasses, embarrassed that I hadn't thought of it before. I held out my hand and said, "Please, take these. I should have offered sooner."

She threw her head back and laughed, hooted actually. I looked around at all the women nearby who had stopped their work to look our way. Nyuziana reached for the glasses and put them on, much to her co-workers' delight. Laughter filled the sun-drenched air as she flitted her head back and forth to show off the glasses. She must have caught my amused look for she quickly removed the glasses and handed them back.

She patted my arm and said, "That was fun. I never had *muzungu* glasses on before, or any glasses. I thank you for the offer, but you saw we would never get work done if I wore these. Laughter would own us."

Before resuming her bent-over labor she said, "*Asante sana* – thank you. You just proved that although I'm black and you are white, we are the same woman, looking for ways to help others."

Laughter owned us all for the rest of the afternoon. I walked from *shamba* to *shamba*, sharing my white person glasses with each woman. The fact that this simple gesture produced so much fun and I'm sure created a topic of conversation for months to come, humbled me. We left the water as the sun began to set. I offered to carry one end of the heavy bags of saturated seaweed plopped on Nyuziana's head.

She accepted immediately, and we walked slowly along the beach, surrounded by women hooting and laughing as they shared their sunglass stories. Some patted me on the back as they swept past, heavy loads on their heads, others grabbed my hand for a second, and I knew that Nyuziana's words were right — we are the same woman. It was clear that I was part of the group, not the tourist hanging out. A giant smile radiated from my face, like the sky changing hues in the setting sun.

Walking back along the beach, the sky burst into a golden bowl, and I walked with a spring in my step. I was happy for me and my new friends, but I was happiest about their new opportunities. It's great to see small business enterprises that women can get involved in. The combination of less physical demand and monetary reward is a rare combination for African women. It makes sense to me that on Zanzibar, the island of my dreams, life is getting better for women through seaweed *shambas* — farms of the sea.

HUMBLED
Jaffa, Sudan
1996

Zooming across the Sahara Desert in an air-conditioned Land Rover, I watched the endless sands of Sudan roll away. Suddenly an unexpected line of women carrying heavy, swaying water containers on their heads appeared from behind a low-slung sand dune. They strutted in the heat and the dust of the open desert plains, 98 percent of them with a baby on their back. And all of them laughing or singing. It was humbling.

These women were the living example of "making the best of a difficult situation." Even in the harshest of conditions, with no transportation choices or options, and endless hard work, they laughed or sang or joked their way through the day, living a true community-based existence.

Life as a rural African woman is beyond difficult. We spent 19 years in Africa, with the Peace Corps and CARE. We went to places not on roads or maps, where every day is a struggle. Where the women keep the villages going — through their hard work and dedication to family.

Women living in the scattered villages we visited explained how they spent more money buying water in a year than buying food. How they grew sorghum and millet, producing enough to feed their families.

One old woman, with a face wrinkled from age and too much sun, told us, "We grow groundnuts and sesame as our cash crops."

If they got good rains the family may make $250 in a productive harvest year. That's about $1.46 a day, for families of six or seven. Food, water, school fees and school uniforms all come from this money. And all of it is earned by the women.

Women are the backbone of Africa. Every day they collect firewood, haul water, hoe fields, beat laundry, pound grain, cook the meals, feed the children and men, and most importantly, make sure their children go to school. And all on less than $1.50 a day.

For years, I thought development programs should be focused on women, rather than men, for a more responsible response. The village of Jaffa proved just that.

On the day we visited, a sea of beautiful women sat on prayer mats beneath the large thorn tree growing in the square of the village of mud huts. The women were ready to hold a meeting.

A CARE project had recently begun, and the women

were boisterous and had gathered to learn how they could receive what we would consider very small loans to start their own income-generating projects. They were there because they had been offered an opportunity to improve their families' lives. An opportunity that no African woman, no matter how busy she already was, would refuse.

It was a social event as well as a meeting. The women were a beautiful array of skin tones and cloth colors, features and jewelry. A few wore gold nose rings, while some others had gold bangles or a necklace. Each wore yards of stunning cloth wrapped around their bodies and draped over their heads. They were dressed in their very finest, as if going to a wedding.

The social gathering ended when the same old wizened woman we had spoken to earlier called it to order. She clapped her hands and soon all the women clapped, then suddenly it stopped with a resounding silence.

The women, dressed for a party, got right down to business. First item on their agenda was to select a Board of Directors for their new organization. They had the unusual distinction of having six literate women amongst them, so no men were needed for the board. A series of ululations filled the air.

Next, they elected a treasurer. The woman chosen told everyone that she could not read or write, so maybe she wasn't the best choice. But the women reassured her that she had been elected because they all had faith and confidence in her honesty. She humbly accepted the position.

The floor then opened to the members to discuss what businesses they would start. One group would be buying chickens and selling eggs. Another group wanted to make candles. Some wanted to buy cloth to sell in the market, and a few hoped to buy a donkey and cart to charge for delivering water. The ideas flowed, and the energy built as plans were made that would add hours to their already full work days. Hours that might take them into the $2-a-day category. The group leader silenced the women again for another announcement.

Two CARE fieldworkers spoke of the seeds and tools program the women were already involved in. Seeds for millet and sorghum were provided, along with hoes. In exchange, the women had to build storage units to house the seeds they got from their harvest plus repay the seed bank for their original loan. As a result, they would each have a bigger harvest and build their own personal seed banks. The ululations erupted when they learned that their women's group had already repaid 93 percent of their loan, while the village men in the same program had repaid only 33 percent.

"GO WOMEN!" I shouted out. The women cheered my encouragement, even though they didn't understand English, they did understand my enthusiasm.

I felt like I had received a huge gift — for their joy had become mine. As I thought about their labor-intensive days in one of the harshest environments in the world, I also thought about how these women turn the most difficult daily challenges into as much fun as possible. They worked together, and struggled together, and celebrated together. Life's challenges were just life and making each day as positive as possible involved working together, singing and joking.

Just about sunset I received an amazing, touching gift. Three women came into the compound where we were staying. They had walked two hours from Jaffa. As a sign of solidarity, they brought me a fried chicken and 11 hardboiled eggs, showing me that no matter how different our lives may be, we are still all connected. These women, amongst the poorest in the world, taught me lessons by their daily approach to life that I will never forget. Lessons we can all benefit from.

We hugged and slapped hands, and then they got a huge surprise. The car drove up that I had been using for days. I opened the back door and they climbed in — laughing and poking each other and feeling the air conditioner — a first I'm sure. We waved as they drove away, and it was impossible to know who was happier. Me, with the surprise visit of appreciation for my enthusiastic outburst during the meeting, or them, in an air-conditioned car that would get them home in 30 minutes.

THE AMAZING SHITAYE AND MUMITA
Addis Ababa, Ethiopia
1998

In every country we lived in I had a different profession. I had been an undercover spy for the Star Travel Service when we lived in Indonesia. I stayed in five-star hotels, wherever I was traveling. Any hotel that could pass the Noise Patrol's stringent criteria would definitely get five stars. I evaluated hotels in Bali, Jakarta, Lombok, the Northern Territory of Australia, Sri Lanka, (where we stayed in Graham Greene's favorite room) and Bangladesh. That morphed into writing the monthly "Feature" and "Teaser" articles for an in-house magazine for a five-star hotel in Jakarta, the Sari Pacific Hotel. That took me all over the islands, and I thought I would never have a better J-O-B.

When we moved to Ethiopia in 1998, opportunities appeared that I could never have dreamt of. My life changed. I met two amazing Ethiopian women early in our two-year stay there, Rahel Mekuria and Shitaye Astawes. They in turn introduced me to many more amazing women, including Mumita Gashew, who still brings a smile to my face and an amazed shake of my head all these years later.

Rahel, Shitaye and I immediately and naturally formed a team that was formidable. We started our own organization called Women on Wheels (WOW) and got 3,020 Ethiopian women off the ground, into their first wheelchairs. That was a major WOW! We also started the first women's magazine in Ethiopia, focused on all issues important to women, from health to harmful traditional practices, professional women and women in education.

Our magazine was called *Women to Women*, written by and for Ethiopians. We were a free, bi-lingual magazine addressing social issues. Our goal was to provide access to information to the most remote and rural women around the country. Rahel Mekuria was the Gender Officer at the British Council and a fast friend. She was the Editor-in-Chief. Mulumebet Zenebe, a professor at the University of Addis Ababa was our Amharic Editor. I was the English Editor and photographer. We had a woman layout artist, and two sisters who ran a printing plant produced the magazine. We rocked. It is without a doubt the thing I am most proud of in my writing career.

Rahel, Mulu and I worked well together. In fact, Rahel and I had started Women on Wheels (WOW) with another amazing woman, Shitaye Astawes, the Women's Program Director of the Ethiopian National Association of the Physically Handicapped. Currently, she is the Executive Director of ENAPH — Ethiopian National Association of Persons with Disabilities. In 1988, she joined us at the magazine as the writer of all the articles on handicapped issues. She was also a moving force in our Women on Wheels project, a subject very close to her heart.

Shitaye has severe rheumatoid arthritis, but that did not slow her down. She was a little tornado. She told me how when she was 12 her pain and diagnosis came as a shock. One day she was a top school student and the next day bedridden. She spent five years in her bedroom in her parents' house. And not once in those five years did her father open the door or go in to see her. He told all who would listen that he did not make sick children. Obviously out of sight, out of mind.

Fortunately for Shitaye, she had an uncle who just stormed into her room one day and said, "You have been here for five years. Do you expect to stay here forever? You were the best student your school had ever seen. And now, you just lie here?"

He turned to leave then stopped at the door and turned

back to say, "Be ready tomorrow morning when I come to get you for school."

The challenges were immense, but Shitaye's new determination was greater. Going out in public with a tiny, misshapen body, filled with pain, was a major challenge, but she went to school that next morning. That day set her free, for she eventually attended university and earned a Master's Degree. When we met she was the Director of Women's Projects for the Ethiopian Handicapped Association. She was tough and took no nonsense from anyone. She now has two children, something she was warned not to do by her doctor.

Being Shitaye she did what she wanted. Her voice was always strong and determined, a characteristic I was experiencing a lot as my circle of Ethiopian women friends grew. If she didn't agree with you, you knew it right away, and if she did it was equally evident. We fought once, when she refused to take one of the 3,000 wheelchairs we brought in. I won though, and she thanked me one day, with the quickest of smiles on her beautiful face.

I was surrounded by amazing women, and the best part was that working on *Women to Women* continuously brought more incredible women into my world. Our first issue was focused on fistula. Fistula in Ethiopia is mainly caused by prolonged, obstructed labor. A fistula is a hole between the vagina and bladder, or vagina and rectum. This results in a constant leak of urine, feces, or both. Fistula is 100% preventable. It's a medical condition, not a disease. It's a trauma. The other three main causes are sexual intercourse between a girl and a man due to early marriage, rape, or surgical complications. Ninety-seven percent of the patients are rural women and girls, victims of the first two causes. The remaining three percent are surgery victims from Addis Ababa.

In 1974, the only fistula hospital in Africa, and possibly the world, opened its doors in Addis Ababa. In 1959, Drs. Catherine and Reginald Hamlin arrived in Ethiopia from Australia. As gynecologists, they immediately began to tackle the huge fistula problem. Word of their successful surgeries spread, and women began to arrive from everywhere. Soon it was clear that the women needed a hospital of their own so the Hamlins started one.

In 1999, Dr. Catherine told me, "We figure for every woman who gets here, at least 10 die on the way. We get about 2,500 patients a year for our 110 beds. We've cured 17,000 women since 1974."

Today, the organization of Hamlin Fistula Ethiopia
oversees the Addis Ababa Fistula Hospital and its five
regional centers, plus the Hamlin College of Midwives, and
the Hamlin Rehabilitation and Reintegration Training
Centre. By 2017, the five regional centers have cured more
than 50,000 women.

That's as amazing as their 90 percent cure rate. A
simple fistula requires an hour-long operation. More
difficult cases can require six hours. Up to 3 percent
cannot be cured at all because the damage is so great. Some
young women arrive with no bladder and others with major
ruptures. These women will always leak, and therefore,
cannot go home. They stay permanently at the center that
helped them. They are greatly valued and appreciated
because they stay on as staff and get to live a meaningful
and positive life helping other victims. Their common
experience with the patients is invaluable.

Mumita Gashew must be the most amazing woman I
have met on this planet. Her personal injuries were so bad
that she was one of the women who couldn't be helped,
and so she stayed to work in the hospital. She's a sturdy
and busy woman, with an instant smile for everyone. But
watch out — she gets done what she plans to, letting

nothing or no one get in her way.

"I am determined to give every woman who comes here love, support and then a kiss goodbye."

She told me her story very matter-of-factly.

"I, Mumita, was married-off at 12 and pregnant at 14."

She endured a four-day labor that produced a stillborn boy and left her a fistula patient.

"Not only did I lose a baby, but my whole life. I became an outcast," she stated bluntly. "It is what still happens to women with fistulas."

Her husband kicked her out because she smelled. Her family didn't want her either, so they locked her in a shed. All her friends avoided her.

"You're spoiled,' they told me through the walls. "No one will ever want you now."

It broke my heart when this strong, sweet woman said sadly, "My shame was great."

She's not sure how long she was in the shed, but one day a woman knocked on the locked door and said, "Listen. You must get out of there and go to the Addis Ababa Fistula Hospital. I will ask for the key and promise to get you on your way. I have also been an outcast in my village, until another woman sent me to the hospital. Go," she told Mumita.

Ruptured, leaking, ashamed, and detested, Mumita walked for two days to the nearest road, then spent three days on a bus. People complained about her but for some reason the bus driver took pity on her and didn't kick her off. (Maybe he had a fistula victim in his family…). Upon her arrival in the teeming Addis Ababa, Mumita found a haven — a hospital with beautiful grounds, loving staff, professional surgeons, and women recovering from fistulas.

Mumita was a woman that was damaged beyond repair, and it was apparent to all that she would never leave the hospital. One afternoon she told me about her life at the hospital. Her story took me from humbled, to humbled and amazed. She spoke with joy as she described her life

"After I recovered from my surgery, I began working as a janitor, cleaning the rooms and common areas here at the hospital. Eventually, I worked up to kitchen staff."

The hospital workers noticed that she had a great way with the patients and were surprised to learn that she had taught herself six very different languages, so she could comfort and encourage the women.

"How else could I help if we couldn't talk?" she said, like everyone just learns six new languages to assist others.

With a wide smile that totally replaced her sadness of moments before she told me, "My best day was when they asked me to work in the operating room. I sterilized the tools and prepared the room and cleaned it afterwards. After a few years, I was allowed to assist the doctors, handing them their tools and actually watching the operations."

What evolved was amazing. After two years of watching and observing the procedures, Mumita corrected a young inexperienced doctor during an operation, saving the patient's life.

Upon discussing this with Mumita, the doctors discovered that she actually had an idea to improve the procedure. They tried it and realized she was correct. Eventually Mumita began training young doctors, teaching them the finer skills and techniques necessary for successful operations. Everything she knew was based upon observation and experience.

I was dazzled by this humble woman's matter-of-fact description of her life that took her from a shed to performing in an operating theater. I thought I had heard it all until she jumped up from the table and said, "I must go. I am late."

"Do you have a class to teach?" I asked.

"Oh no," she said proudly. "I have a class to attend. I am learning to read and write!"

WOW
Addis Ababa, Ethiopia
1998

The day I met Rahel Mekuria was a game-changer in my life. I had been hired by the British Council to teach a short story writing workshop for local women. We were going to work together on the workshop, and after a quick introduction we got down to business.

"Are you a writer?" Rahel asked. I said yes and asked the same about her.

With a wide smile she said, "Not yet, but I will be when the workshop is done." And in that instant, we both knew that a great friendship was on the horizon.

I met Rahel in 1998, and she had already lived a professional lifetime. She is hailed as "the woman who pioneered broadcasting education" in Ethiopia. After completing her studies at Homerton College in Cambridge, United Kingdom, she returned to Addis ready to pursue her passion of leading and sharing simultaneously.

"I am passionate about being a lending hand for others," she's quoted as saying.

Before we met she had worked for 30 years with the Ethiopian Ministry of Education. She started the first

English-language education program on Ethiopian TV in 1965, directing and performing for Reading Rainbow.

She had been Deputy Chairperson for the Peace and Development Organization. And if that wasn't enough, she also served on the Elders Council, made up of various NGOs that worked for peace.

She's proud of that because, "The Council was instrumental in the release of political prisoners."

Being with her in 1998 was like being with a rock star. Just about everywhere we went people often stopped her to say that she taught them how to read.

Later, I even met a taxi driver in D.C. who was a big fan of Rahel. When I mentioned that I had lived in Ethiopia he was happy but unimpressed. When I mentioned I had worked with Rahel he became effusive, saying that the first book he ever heard read, *Green Eggs and Ham*, was on her program. At the end of the ride he charged me nothing, he was so thankful to hear that Rahel was well and still making a difference.

As the head of the Educational Television Production Division with the Educational Media agency she was overseeing basically everything — from preparing scripts to production work to securing funding to running a camera.

Both she and the program thrived under her leadership.

From there she became the Executive Director of YWCA/Ethiopia. Under her guidance for five years the YWCA became a moving force in promoting women's rights in Ethiopia. Education and women's empowerment were major focuses of the YWCA under Rahel's leadership.

When asked what enables a woman to thrive she said, "When she is given the opportunity to access education, knowledge, and knows her rights." And Rahel has dedicated her life to these objectives.

When we met that first day I didn't know any of this, just that she was the Gender Officer for the British Council and worked on women's programs. We connected from the very beginning and went on to accomplish some amazing things together.

The first workshop we did for 10 women was nothing like the British Council expected. I asked Rahel if we could do it in my front garden instead of in the sterile, depressing room at the British Council. She said in her typical cheerful fashion, "I don't see why not."

Then we strategically placed copies of Ms. Magazine around my living room, which all the participants picked up and read during the breaks.

On the last day they announced, "We don't want to make a book of short stories, we want to start a women's magazine." And so "Women to Women" or "*Seytoch le Seytoch*" was born.

It took nine months to get everything in place. Amazingly the funding was the easiest part. The British Council in Addis and Cambridge University Press put up the money. Then began the writing process. None of the women were trained journalists, and neither Rahel nor I had ever started a magazine before. Getting articles together on a range of topics like health, education, professional women, plus a short story and a poem (the only thing not translated) was a major challenge. We also had a debate page, always addressing both sides of a sensitive issue, and a section called "A Day in the Life Of" where any woman could write about a topic of her choice from her life. I can't imagine making this happen with anyone other than Rahel, for she knew everyone, was respected by all, and was a joy to work with.

Twice a year for four years, we printed 2,500 copies. They were distributed free to rural women around the country. With a literacy rate of only 29 percent it was important to put the magazine where the most women could see it and where a literate woman or girl could read to others.

Clinics were a perfect place. We also gave it to 235 schools, universities, trade schools, and secondary institutions. It was funny because we started getting complaint letters from men, calling the magazine "gender insensitive" for its title. We both got a good laugh out of that.

With her eyes shining Rahel told me, "That means we're doing it right, my friend.

"Women to Women" is the thing I am most proud of in my writing career, but what followed next was even more incredible.

When the workshop was completed and the magazine running smoothly, Rahel looked at me with that familiar glint in her eyes and said, "Remember what Shitaye told us — about do a lot or do nothing at all — for handicapped women? So, how do we do a lot?"

Inspired by the challenge, I got on the Internet to explore. Internet service was sporadic at best in Addis Ababa in 1998, but I began my search for free wheelchairs.

Our goal was to get as many women off the ground as possible. The first group I found was Joanie And Friends

Ministries (JAF). After several emails back and forth, they eventually said they would send 20 wheelchairs, but we had to get them from Tennessee to Ethiopia. When I told Rahel and Shitaye about the 20 chairs, I volunteered to do the States part, though I had no idea how. Shitaye took on the D.C. to Ethiopia task, confident as ever. Rahel would handle customs in her diplomatic style.

Shitaye contacted Ethiopian Airlines on behalf of Ethiopian National Association for the Physically Handicapped, (ENAPH) and they agreed to fly the chairs to Addis for free, once they reached D.C. Rahel had all the necessary paperwork from ENAPH and arranged custom-free entry status. But none of that could happen until transport was set-up in the U.S. — and I had made no head-way. So, I made a rare long-distance phone call from Ethiopia to my sister Dianne Warren in Sarasota, Fla., for help. She jumped right on board and Women On Wheels became four strong women.

Dianne asked her "go to" neighbor, Bill, if he had any ideas. He shocked her when he said, "Hey, my best friend is the Transportation Director in Tennessee."

Amazingly, two days later the wheelchairs were picked up from the prison where inmates had a program to rehab used wheelchairs. Three days later, 20 chairs were delivered directly to the D.C. warehouse of Ethiopian Airlines, and arrived in Addis Ababa six days later.

Rahel was at the airport when they arrived, and in her calm, organized style, she got the chairs through customs without a hitch. That was a major accomplishment, given the bureaucratic nightmare Ethiopia is famous for being. I am sure to this day that only Rahel could make such a project so trouble-free. Even feisty Shitaye couldn't believe that it had all happened so smoothly, not to mention the unbelievable speed of it all.

Rahel and I personally delivered the first 20 chairs from JAF Ministries in 1999, in one day. It was an honor to see the first 20 women get off the ground. Two months after distribution, Rahel and I visited two recipients, to see if their wheelchairs had changed their lives.

Merim Muhammad, 37, had been paralyzed for 36 years. She smiled brightly from the comfort of her wheelchair. As she knitted a sweater from the cotton she had spun she told us, "I can visit little stores and go to church. I can sit in the sun without having to ask anyone to carry me there. My wheelchair gives me great happiness."

Her sister bragged, "She has become an activist,

speaking out at the Kebele about housing and programs for handicapped people." Merim's new self-confidence radiated off her in waves.

My favorite moment was with Mamitu Tefera. She was an active third-grader when she suddenly lost the use of her legs. We found her sitting proudly in her classroom, a happy 18-year-old student resuming her studies — in the third grade.

"I can finish my education," she said with pride. "And now I am free to explore the world. I have been to the zoo and the Piazza to look in the store windows." Patting the arms of her wheelchair she said, "You thought you gave me wheels, but you really gave me wings."

Pumped by our success, Shitaye, Rahel and I joined hands. With her "what's next?" glint in her eyes, Rahel asked, "And now, ladies, how do we get more chairs?" So back to the Internet I went.

The next big find was the Wheelchair Foundation in Blackburn, Calif. They had a goal of giving away 1 million wheelchairs in five years. I contacted them and that began a process that drifted over the next four years. They quickly promised us chairs — but could not say when. For a year, erratic emails passed back and forth between California and

Ethiopia, but still no delivery date.

In 1999, Joe and I moved across the African continent to Mali. The wheelchair challenge moved with me. I didn't want to let my Ethiopian friends down, and I really didn't want to risk losing any wheelchairs.

Mali had bigger communication challenges than Ethiopia, so once again I called my sister Dianne and asked, "Can you be my voice? Can you please call Fred at The Wheelchair Foundation?"

She got on the job, and established a good relationship with them, but still there was no set date. Two years later we moved to St. John in the Caribbean, and still we were working on the wheelchairs. In 2001, the incredible happened when Dianne and I were invited to join Ted Behring, the founder of the Wheelchair Foundation, and several donors, on his private jet to deliver wheelchairs in Africa and Europe. We were invited because we never gave up.

It was the trip of a lifetime — seven countries in 10 days. At each stop, we presented a symbolic 100 chairs representing the 1500 that were on the way. Ethiopia was our third stop, after Nigeria and Tanzania. And there, standing on the runway to greet us, was Rahel. She had arranged ground transport for us and for the off-loading of the 100 chairs into a truck for delivery the next morning. Dianne and I couldn't hug her enough. She had made arrangements for the airport to be open and customs present when we arrived. Once our passports were stamped, she led us to a waiting hotel bus where she welcomed us to Ethiopia. In true gracious Rahel fashion, she thanked us for letting her be a small part of such a life-changing event.

Nothing is easy in Ethiopia, especially when it involves the government. So, I was shocked when our troubles began in the States. Before starting the trip, confusion reigned. The Mormons, who are a major contributor to the Wheelchair Foundation, didn't realize that the chairs were meant for the Women's Wing of ENAPH. They had contacted USAID in Ethiopia who immediately decided to give them away — to men.

I was not happy and called Gary, Director of Philanthropy for the Mormons in Salt Lake City. I knew that a long time had passed since I had started this project because our contact was a conference call between Gary in Utah, Fred on a trip to Mexico and me in St. John, something not possible in my Ethiopia or Mali days. The

Mormons, sorry for the mix-up, promised to provide 1,500 chairs matching the Wheelchair Foundation's donation. Eventually WOW got 3,000 women off the ground. WOW! There's probably no better sight than the joy on a person's face when they sit in their own wheelchair for the first time in their life.

After Ethiopia, we took wheelchairs to Egypt, Jordan, Romania and Ukraine. Again, and again I got to witness the jubilation of recipients and family members. And when I think about Mumita Tefera's words, I know that Rahel gave me wings too. I have never met a more respected, dedicated, adored and humble community activist and leader in my professional or personal life. That day we first met we both knew that we were going to be a team, but never did we imagine that our magazine "Women to Women" or Women on Wheels (WOW) would be our contributions to Ethiopia.

In 2014, the Association of Women in Business in Addis Ababa awarded Rahel the "Abled Woman of Excellence Award". The award recognizes outstanding community leaders who make a difference. If that is not Rahel I don't know who is.

THREE FACES OF FANTU
Remote Mali
1999

We were sitting on the banks of the Niger River, two days from Bamako, the capitol city of Mali. Twenty-five men from five villages sat on mats, some sitting up-right, and others stretched out, balancing on bent elbows with dirty feet pointing out.

Ten CARE people sat on plastic string chairs, tipping precariously on the uneven hard-packed ground. Fatimata and I were the only women present, until she appeared.

She looked old, 60 plus I would guess. She was dressed in a brown and beige *pagne*, or cloth wrap. She had no top on, and her boobs sagged like deflated boda bags. I'd never seen a topless woman in a Muslim village before. She looked around at the crowd gathered, then marched right into the empty center space, standing upright between the village men and the CARE workers. No one paid her the slightest bit of attention as she bent and spoke or shouted earnestly into each visitor's face — black, white, man or woman.

"Don't look at her," Fatimata told me. "Pretend she isn't there."

"How old is she?" I asked as the woman marched off in a huff.

"Old, very old. More than 40 but less than 50. Very old."

"Same as me," I told Fatimata.

My friend shook her head and said between long loud sucks of her teeth, "*Ce n'est pas la même chose* — it's not the same thing — American years and African years."

I had to agree. "Have you seen her before?"

"Every time we are here," replied Fatimata. "She is called Fantu."

The meeting, which had not lost a beat during Fantu's visit, was still going strong. Fatimata translated from Bambara to French for me, while Sitibay translated for Joe. The men were discussing their villages' progress in their CARE program of building sluice dams for their rice fields on the river. Two men were raising their voices at one another when, as suddenly as she had left, Fantu re-emerged from the dusty alley that ran between two mud huts.

She was wearing a whole new look, nothing like she had worn before. Fantu had on a brilliant orange *pagne*, with a flowing matching blouse. Her head was wrapped in a white cloth that gave it shape, and then a matching bright orange cloth was elaborately tied around the white cloth. She was looking fine! Much to my shock and dismay, the final touch was a bright orange whistle, which she promptly blew shrilly. She looked directly at me and blew a sharp staccato rift on her tin whistle, as if she knew that one of my nicknames is Noise Patrol.

"Don't look at her," Fatimata warned me. "If she gets a reaction from you, you will be sorry."

I dropped my eyes to the ground and fought the urge to put my hands over my ears. While staring at the ground I noticed the large calabash gourd she had set at her feet. Blasting on her whistle like a berserk playground director, she stooped to pick up the calabash that was full of things. She carried her gourd of goodies to the edge of the men's group, and like a kid at show and tell, or a magician on a stage, she pulled things out, one by one.

First was a cooking pot, then an old wooden spoon with half of its face missing. With the flick of her wrist she beat on the metal cooking pot with her broken spoon. That was bad but when the whistle joined in the noise was deafening. And still no one paid her any attention. She even threw in a few dance steps.

The goodie display continued. It looked like the head of an old mop suddenly appeared with a flourish. And then strangest of all, an old Coca Cola bottle encrusted with dirt. A very unusual sight to see out in the middle of nowhere, long after the Coke bottles were made. I immediately thought of The Gods Must Be Crazy. She took a few giant swigs of nothing from the bottle, the whole time watching to see who was watching her. Fortunately, I sat behind her, so I was free to stare.

"I think she is drinking for courage," whispered Fatimata.

Fantu dropped the dirty old bottle back into the gourd, then began clapping and whistling as she shuffled into the empty space between the two groups. As she danced and sang with an occasional whistle blast she moved in front of each visitor, demanding attention. Joe dropped his head to look at his shoes when she reached him. Obviously Sitibay had warned him against any eye contact. She clapped and whistled and stamped and sang, and still received no attention.

The village men carried on in Bambara about water levels and rice production, and the CARE people carried on with simultaneous translation about village committees and yields. And all the while, Fantu danced and sang and demanded attention — but got none. With a final stamp of her foot, she re-loaded her gourd of goods and left.

Fatimata leaned towards me and said, "She's not normal. In fact, she is crazy. Maybe now she is gone." She shook her head and said, "We don't lock our crazies away, which is good, I think?"

"Is she dangerous?" I asked.

"Sometimes," came the answer. "Especially when the meeting is inside. Then she will break down the door."

The talking continued. "This many hectare and that much water produces this many baskets of rice…" and, "We are starting a seed bank like you showed us…" All business as usual. As the voices droned the third face of Fantu appeared, from another alley and directly behind the village men.

The brilliant orange *pagne* was gone, replaced by a brown one, with a huge beige flower design located right across her butt. She also wore a stylish ruffled top and matching head tie. She had the gourd again, with the handle of a large axe sticking out the top.

I tried not to watch as she took the axe from the gourd and shook it at us over the men's heads. She then walked briskly around the men and down to the water's edge behind me. I tried to ease forward inconspicuously, ready to run if Fatimata gave me a signal to flee. Fatimata tilted her head, as if to say "Look!" I turned and watched as Fantu pushed her gourd, loaded with the axe, into the narrow but deep river.

With each step she descended into deeper water until the only things visible were her gourd and axe handle, the top of her head, and a raised fist — clearly telling us that we all sucked. A few men chuckled when she emerged on the other side of the narrow offshoot of the Niger River she had just crossed. Glancing over her soggy shoulder she looked at the group as if to say, "Gotcha! You're all looking now."

Without a care in the world, she checked on her axe and gourd, then headed for the sparse forest nearby.

"Good," said Fatimata. "Let her chop wood and not us. She was angry because no one would acknowledge her." Smoothing her gown, she said, "If we had she would still be here, singing and dancing and blowing her whistle."

Just before disappearing from sight, Fantu turned and looked directly at me. I nodded in recognition of her show and determination and we shared a smile. The mischievous glint in her eye shone even from the distance that separated us. As she walked into the bush I could only think, I wish I was that free!

RESPECT
Bamako, Mali
2000

Noise Patrol. That's what my husband Joe and closest friends call me. It perfectly reflects my personality and is the bane of my existence. I once told a friend, "I think I was standing in the dog line when God gave out ears." I hate it.

The slightest whirrrrr of a cricket in a house the size of a football field drives me crazy. The relentless tick of Joe's clock, tucked safely in a drawer, can keep me awake. The sound of a neighbor's radio or television drives me bonkers, so imagine my madness when I realized we had moved next door to a "tap-tap" woman in Bamako, Mali.

Bamako was to be my salvation after a trying time in Addis Ababa. We had just left Ethiopia where I had been certifiably deranged for the last seven months by a massive construction project 15 feet from my office wall. For two years and five months the house had been in an idyllic location in a bustling city — quiet, beautiful, at the very end of a small dirt road. All of that changed in the skip of a heartbeat.

Suddenly, there was an endless stream of earth movers

and rock smashers, trucks and workers, who found ample time to sit in a tree and stare over the wall. The noise took over my life, and when it kicked into seven days a week before the rains began in earnest, I almost committed Hari Kari off the wall, in front of a sellout crowd of workers. The only thing that kept me remotely sane was knowing that we were moving, across Africa, far from the all-consuming noise next door.

The house in Bamako, Mali, had been the organization's director's house for at least six years, so it was ready for us when we arrived. It was located at the end of a very wide, bumpy, dirt road. Three games of pick-up soccer could happen simultaneously, and directly opposite the house was a sand pile as big as a Saharan dune. It was the end of the line for water, electricity and phone, although a sprawling village lived just beyond it.

If you didn't stop in front of our house you'd drive right into a gully. Houses were built in the dry riverbed, and then knocked down by the rains every year. There was a thriving village community going on across the usually dry divide.

Before arriving, I was incessant, asking Joe, "Do we have neighbors?" "Could anyone come in and start building

95

next to us?" "How close is the nearest mosque?" They were just my standard Noise Patrol questions, heightened by my paranoia after living those seven months in my very worst nightmare — on a construction site.

"No problem," Joe assured me. "I've been told that there's only one woman living on a small plot next to the house, on the edge of the dry stream bed. She makes *gri-gri* packets to sell. No problem."

I believed him — for the first four weeks. Then it quickly became clear that the neighbor did more than just make *gri-gri* packets, the little sachets people wear stuffed with herbs or animal parts or lines from the Koran to give them protection from *ju-ju* — black magic, or to find a husband or have a baby.

It was on a Monday afternoon, during Week 5, when all hell broke loose. The day started with its usual massive blue skies and street sounds. There was the barber walking by clicking his scissors, looking for business, and the garbage man on his donkey cart yelling for people to get their trash out, if it wasn't already. There was no car traffic, and no construction, and I was in hog heaven. Just birds and wind in the trees and bushes, and an overwhelming sense of peace and quiet.

"This is just what the doctor ordered," I told Joe at breakfast. He released a major sigh of relief. It had to have been tough surviving the madness of Ms. Menopausal Noise Patrol on the Rampage in Addis Ababa. Finally, I was calm.

That Monday afternoon, I chatted with Robert in our kitchen in my fumbling rusty French. He worked in the house and loved to talk. We were laughing about my painful accent as I tried to tell him how much I loved the peace and quiet, when suddenly a tremendous noise started. Crashing through the walls and wrapping itself around us was a cacophony that sounded like an angry mob banging hubcaps with metal rods.

Eyes wide, terror etching lines in my face, I stammered, "What the hell is that?!" in English, for my French had totally failed me.

Robert shook his head slowly and said, "It's our neighbor, doing her work."

I stood stunned, in what was supposed to be our kitchen for years to come, overwhelmed by the bangings getting more frenetic — and then wailing women joined in. It was the sound of fingernails being torn out, or hot cigarettes being pressed against sensitive parts. It ripped the peaceful afternoon as effectively as a giant fart in a silent church.

As if in a trance, I followed the noise out the front gate and to the right. Peering around the corner of the wall I saw only a man and woman sitting outside a hut that stood a foot from our wall. They looked like two people watching a movie, not talking, or anything, just looking in the same direction. They also looked oblivious to the wailing and the banging, like it was just business as usual.

I didn't know what to do. They would never hear my shouts over the ruckus blasting out from behind them, the source hidden by the tilted mud hut. It crossed my mind again that they looked like people at a drive-in, both watching something out of my sight. I shook my head in defeat and returned home.

For four solid afternoons, the screeching and the hubcap abuse continued, and when I was finally strung out to my very last nerve I announced to Joe, "We have to move."

"What?" he asked, looking defeated and bummed out.

"We have to move," I said again. "Madame Tap-Tap was here first, and I don't want to mess with the sounds coming out of there. It's intense, and it says to me, loud and clear, DON'T MESS WITH ME!"

Joe shook his head and said, "Fine."

"I feel as if I've turned in 100 happy workers staring over the wall for 10 frenzied bangers. I don't want to mess with what she's doing so we have to move. How did what's his name live here?" I asked. "Didn't it drive him crazy? Or his partner crazy?"

"He was alone, and never here during the afternoon. So, I guess he never knew."

"Well, I'm here and we're moving," I said.

The next morning, before the banging began, I asked Robert, "What is she doing over there? It doesn't sound friendly."

"Women come to her to contact the gods when they are sick, or searching for a husband for their daughters, or want a job. And sometimes it's not so nice," he said. He was reluctant to go on, but finally added, "Basically, for any problem that can be solved by a little donation, she will dance, and wail, and bang away."

"We have to move," I told Joe again that night.

I know that I am very lucky to be married to the picture of patience. Knowing that I — no we — had barely survived the building chaos of Addis he went to the office the next day and told Diop (Jope), the man dealing with houses, "We need to move."

Diop was shocked, "But why? It's a beautiful house."

"Go talk to my wife," was all Joe said.

Diop arrived at the house on a banging afternoon and was appalled by the noise.

"We'll make her stop," he said loudly. "This is not the bush. It is the capital city!"

"No," I said. "I don't want to mess with the woman or what she is doing. It just sounds too powerful and not particularly positive."

A loud wail punctuated my sentence, and the banging kicked into double-time. Diop's eyes grew wide and he said, "I agree, it does not sound friendly."

"We'll move," I said, "she was here first."

Diop agreed and the house hunt began.

Bamako is not a big place in a lot of regards, although it is a bustling, populated place. Each day Diop and I looked at available houses, but nothing interested me. After a week of house-hunting, and 15 viewings, the owner of our house showed up at the office.

"*Bonjour*," said the *propriétaire*. "I've heard that you're looking for another house. Is there a problem?"

Diop explained about the noise and the guy said, "Not to worry. I'll deal with it."

Wasting no time, he jumped into his Mercedes Benz and rushed over to our house that he owned. He had built it with *toubabs* (foreigners) in mind, so that they would rent it until he'd paid off the construction. Then he would move his family into the beautiful, fully paid for home. Our neighbor was messing with his plan, and he was not happy.

To say the least I was surprised when he came striding through the gate, a handsome man in a beautiful light green *grand boubou* gown covered with light blue embroidery. He had a fat gold watch on his wrist and looked like someone used to be being in charge.

"*Bonjour madame. Comment ça va?* I am here to take care of the neighbor."

Right away I didn't like him. He was arrogant and definitely pushy. In my pitiful French I said, "Please, don't go over there. I don't want to make the woman angry."

But he didn't listen, instead turning on the heel of his leather sandal and he strode back out the gate. Fortunately, as he was leaving Diop showed up, so they went together. I followed at a reluctant distance. Diop and the landlord found a man, just sitting around his tiny compound, the noise coming from the hut behind him. He was shocked by the sudden arrival of the two well-dressed men. When he recognized the landlord he quickly stood up.

"What is this noise?" the landlord asked rudely, not even being polite enough to greet the man.

"What noise?" he asked. "I hear no noise."

"The banging. And the wailing," continued the landlord.

"You mean my wife's work?" he asked.

"Yes," said Diop. "Does this happen all the time?"

"Oh no," he said. "It only happens one day a week, every Thursday, 2 to 5 p.m."

Diop thanked the man and turned to me. I laughed when they relayed this message to me and said, "Fine, no problem. But there were four Thursdays last week."

That night, the husband of Madame Tap-Tap, sat with our watchman. His wife was not happy and had kicked him out of the hut for the night.

It was also the first time my bedside light self-illuminated in the middle of the night.

1:04 to be exact.

I woke up, the light suddenly shining in my eyes. Reaching out to shut it off, I thought it was strange, but then went back to sleep. I didn't mention it to Joe, until two days later, after my light turned on again by itself in the middle of the night.

1:06 to be exact.

Joe just laughed it off, even though he admitted that our 10-year-old lamps had never self-illuminated before. He laughed until his light went on that night.

1:08 to be exact.

The next morning, I sent the woman six coconuts from our garden, and that night the lights didn't go on. There followed a stream of *petits cadeaux*, little gifts, that I sent around the wall to the woman I'd never met. Local incense was popular, as was a bag of oranges.

When Diop and the owner heard that the husband had been banished from the house for a night, they went back to talk to her — for the woman was clearly in charge.

"She's a tough one," Diop told me. "She says it's only two days a week, Thursday and Friday, 2 to 6 p.m."

"Don't go again, because it'll only be three days a week, 1 to 7, on your third visit," I said. "If there really was a schedule, that would be different because I could leave then. But it can start at any moment, and that is worse." I shook my head in total frustration.

As if that had been a cue, the banging began.

The house hunting was still underway when one day Madame Tap-Tap's son came over. He was about 18, and clearly nervous. "My mother sent me," he said. "She has a bad belly. She wonders, do you have any medicine?"

Not knowing exactly what she had, and not being a stocked pharmacy, I sent our neighbor a papaya from our yard. The boy did not look impressed as I told him, "She must eat a big spoonful of the seeds. It is a cure I learned in the Seychelles."

He took the papaya home, looking almost fearful of what his mother would say. It did the trick. Four hours later he was back to say his mother was feeling much better. It suddenly occurred to me that maybe I had just established some of my own little *ju-ju* reputation.

Life went on. Madame Tap-Tap banged away, and I began to resemble the nut case from Addis Ababa. I stepped up the house hunting. Some days the noise was almost muffled, and I asked Robert why.

"It's because she is inside the closed hut. She is inside because she's calling on devils. When she calls the gods she's outside."

Uh-huh, I thought. I knew not to mess with her.

The house hunt was at a standstill. I'd seen every house available, and not found anything. Fortunately, there was a sudden respite in the afternoon banging sessions.

"Why is she quiet for so many days?" I asked Robert. I was not encouraged by the response.

"It's only temporary," he said, "because no one has money, so she has no business. Wait until after the harvest, then she'll be really busy. Bus loads will come here."

In the meantime, after three months of living in a house where we had unpacked only the basics — music, computer, kitchen things and clothes, I finally told Joe, "Let's unpack and really move in. I'll just keep a casual house hunt up, and when I find something, then we'll move."

"Fine," was all he said.

All the while I was trying to think of a Plan B, for when the noise cranked up again. On one Saturday afternoon, I told Joe, "Maybe I can rent her an office. You know, somewhere farther away, where she can work."

Joe only laughed. It was amusing to imagine her packing up her bangers and telling her husband, "I'm off to the office, dear."

The following Monday I committed myself to the

house by buying seeds to plant a garden for when the veggie season ends in Mali. A garden means you're staying. That day at noon, while the soil was being turned for the garden, Madame Tap-Tap's son came over again.

"My mother knows that you respect her work, so she has spent two nights up, looking for a way for all to live in peace. She has decided to find a place to work away from home…"

"Now she's reading my mind," I told Joe. "You're the only one who knows about Plan B."

Turning back to the young man I said, "I'll pay. I don't want this to cost her anything, and I want to show her how much I appreciate her understanding and looking for a solution."

I didn't mention that I had come up with the same plan already.

The next morning Diop went over to strike the deal. Madame Tap-Tap said she needed $12 a month to rent her space to work.

"Let's give her $20 so she can buy a drum instead of a hubcap. And please tell her I want to be her friend," I told Diop when he went back to see the neighbor.

Diop came back to the house with a big shining smile.

"She's very happy. Especially about being friends."

So, life shifted into a quiet phase, with everyone a happy camper. Joe and I went off to Timbuktu for 10 days. Timbuktu really is out there, a collection of sand buildings dumped in the Sahara Desert. There's a special ambiance to a full-on desert town far from everywhere.

One night we went out into the Sahara to watch the sunset from a sand dune. The space and silence and rolling sand dunes were totally peaceful. Or it was until I stepped on a mega-thorn that drove deep into my foot. We were with a Tuareg guide, who pulled the shaft from my foot and put sand on it to stop the bleeding. When that didn't work, he took out his bag of raw tobacco and packed a dollop of soggy leaves over the wound. It was amazing. The bleeding stopped immediately, and the tobacco also numbed the area, giving me instant pain relief.

I told Joe, "More traditional medicine for the neighbor. This is right up there with the papaya cure. If she ever steps on a thorn and needs help, tobacco to the rescue." As an afterthought I added, "Only problem is she better have her own pouch of raw tobacco."

I was relaxed and happy as we drove the 14 hours back to Bamako. But that came to a screeching halt. We arrived home to a crowd outside the neighbor's small compound, and full speed ahead drumming and shrieking and whistles. I shook my head in dismay, thinking, "O.K., she didn't know we were coming home today. Get a grip, Cristina."

It went 'til midnight that night. A first. Word had it that it would go again the next day, from mid-morning till sunset. It was a special three-day event, and we had missed the first day. The next morning a shocked Diop and *propriétaire* of the house arrived.

"Don't go over there and make her angry," I begged. "It's only one more day."

We had to shout to hear each other over the noise.

"We are going to pay her, in front of everyone. It will be very good for her reputation. Robert says she had to do this at home because the people near her office couldn't take the noise," Diop explained. "They threatened her with violence, so she came home again."

They were gone for quite a while. On their return Diop said, "She was very happy to get the money, and very sorry that this has happened. But she feared for her life and her clients were afraid to go there, too. She promised to be done by sunset," he shouted.

"Can I go watch?" I yelled.

"Oh, she would love that," screamed Diop.

It was a sight I'm not soon to forget. Nor will I forget Diop's repeated, "I am so glad we didn't make her angry!"

Her compound was small, no bigger than a one-car garage, and it was full of women in gowns and head ties of every color imaginable. Backed up against our wall were two men playing long, wooden xylophones called *balafons*. Beside them sat two women, playing bowl-shaped gourds turned upside down in giant tubs of water. The gourds had loosely strung cowrie shell necklaces draped around them, the source of the nerve-racking clacking sound. Each woman beat frantically on the adorned gourds with sturdy sticks.

A small group of women danced in front of the musicians, jerking back and forth, each in their own little world. Madame Tap-Tap made a grand entrance from her hut. She saw me standing in the group outside her compound, a beacon as the lone white woman. Our eyes met for the very first time, as she walked directly over to me. We shook hands as Diop introduced us.

As we held hands and looked into each other's eyes with the intensity of a couple getting married, Madame Tap-Tap began speaking loudly in Bambara, the local language.

"*I ni tileh*," she said.

"She greets you," said Diop.

Then the woman began to talk at length. "She blesses your friendship, and your house," Diop translated, bending down to my ear and shouting. "And she welcomes you to her home."

We smiled widely at one another, I thanked her for being my friend, and then she turned back to her business, and proceeded to show Diop and me her stuff.

She wore a deep, blood red gown and head tie with gold embroidery. With all eyes on her, she moved into the center of the circle.

The banging on the gourds and the *balafons* stopped dead.

Madame stood facing the musicians. At a nod of her head the music started with a very slow, repetitive beat — clack, clack, clack, pause, clack, clack, clack. With her eyes straight ahead, and a look of pure concentration on her face, the woman started a slow backstroke with her arms. Her circles became bigger, and the beat increased.

Keeping up with the growing beat her arms flailed around in a wide, frenetic backwards windmill motion. She maintained the speed for two or three minutes, her eyes never leaving the musicians. Then finally her arms wound down to hang at her sides as all expression left her face. It reminded me of an old chalkboard being wiped clean. She looked empty.

"She has reached the first stage of trance," said Diop. His eyes were wide as he watched.

Madame Tap-Tap didn't stay still for more than a heartbeat when she started moving her head in slow circles on her totally limp neck. Like before, as the beat built up, she kept up. This time it was her neck and head that fought to command the beat. Her frantic head circles moved at a speed that hurt to watch.

"Now this is truly *le vraiment* trance," said Diop. She moved back into the middle of the circle, kicking up little blips of dust as she stamped her feet on the hard, rocky ground, then suddenly she fell in a heap. Her body jerked in little spasms, and all the women rushed forward to pick her up. It was then that the young girl appeared from inside the hut. She moved among the dancing/thrashing/whip-lashing women, past the collapsed woman, and into the middle of the circle.

She looked like a *ju-ju* girl in training, as she repeated all the things her mother had done — frantic backstroke, neck-breaking head roll, and finally falling to the ground. Two women stepped forward and lifted her by the twine belt wrapped around her waist and moved around the circle of sitting women with her limp body. They dipped the head of the rag doll girl into the lap of each woman elder. They each patted her head as she was moved around the circle.

Meanwhile, her mother stood with the help of four women and began talking in tongues. Her head was thrust back, and she spoke to the sky in an insistent, monotone shout. The instruments stopped as if she was waiting for an answer, then began again slowly. As she spoke, women rushed up and rubbed her arms, hoping for contact with the powers she had reached. Many women were dancing themselves into stupors or collapsed heaps looking just like the Whirling Dervishes in Sudan. Diop and I watched in silent awe.

"I have never heard this language before," said Diop. "And I am SO GLAD we didn't make her angry."

When they pulled out the chickens and started slitting throats for an offering and meal, we left.

"Oh, Cristina, you were so right," Diop said as he dried his brow with a cloth pulled from the deep pocket on his gown. "I have never seen anything like this, especially in the city. That is what you find in the bush. She has many powers that we don't want to bother."

The banging went on all afternoon, and twice I went back to watch. On the second visit Madame Tap-Tap was dressed in a dark green gown covered in purple threads. She nodded at me as she suddenly reappeared in her compound. Staring at me as if to say, "Watch this," she tapped the shoulder of one of the women gourd-bangers and sat down to take over. Her arms disappeared in a blur as she drove the beat faster and faster and faster. She didn't let up until the last dancer had collapsed.

On my third visit the *ju-ju* woman was wearing a gold gown with black embroidery. She didn't know I was there, for she was fully tranced. Deep in the throes of her trance she talked and screamed and shook one woman like a limp rag. When she was finished speaking and thrashing, she dropped the woman like a wet towel. I was amazed to see the woman get up and walk away as if she hadn't just been dropped to the ground — limp as a rag doll.

I left when the little girl in her *bogolan* vest jumped back into the center of the circle. For some reason I couldn't express, it really depressed me to see the young girl flailing about, then limp like a rag. It was strange because it amazed me to see the mother — but saddened me to see her kid in action.

Madame Tap-Tap and I lived happily for a while. I thought maybe the three-day event was like a farewell concert at her home. I felt good for her, for her prestige was clear and her powers respected. For five months, until we left for a vacation, the *ju-ju* woman worked quietly, making the *gri-gri* pouches for her customers. Little gifts continued to go over the wall and we supplied the neighbor and her family with water. We would meet from time to time, and shake hands and repeat French and Bambara greetings, but the language barrier prevailed. One day, while shaking hands, Madame Tap-Tap nonchalantly pulled up her sleeve to expose a triple row of *gri-gri* pouches attached to her bicep. A warning of some kind, I wondered? They were bigger than most and I had to wonder what animal parts lurked inside.

We went on vacation to the states, and when we returned home to Bamako, we were very happy — for about two days. On the second afternoon a familiar noise filled the air. It ripped through my office like raging jackhammers, and when the whistles kicked in I nearly began to scream.

Holding my head with both hands I asked Robert, "Is she back at it? Maybe she doesn't know we're back."

Next day, Diop the diplomat made another visit.

The woman awaited his arrival with a stern face and a straight back. "I am sorry," she said, "but my power really is connected to my house and compound. I must work here."

And that was the end of the discussion.

Diop was outraged, but I wasn't. I told Diop, "I have to say, I respect her for saying, 'O.K., I tried it and it didn't work. Now, I'm going back to all my work again, in my home.' I'll just have to live with it, until we find another house."

We still greeted each other whenever we crossed paths, and my little gifts still went over the wall, as did the water supply. She banged and screeched whenever she had customers, and sometimes there were three or four Thursdays in a week. Other weeks had no Thursday or Friday at all. And so, we lived in a short-lived peaceful coexistence, while the house hunting continued.

Thankful for every quiet day, I was happy when we suddenly made the decision to move to the Caribbean. As we packed, I made piles of things to give away — from an exercise bike for Madou, who had diabetes, to a prize pile of goodies for Madame Tap-Tap.

Two days before departing I asked the gardener to invite my neighbor over. He waited outside the front gate, and when Madame was returning home he invited her in. She nodded at him and said, "I am coming."

About 30 minutes later she appeared, dressed in one of her finest *grand boubous*, a deep rich indigo blue with gold embroidery. She came into the screened patio, checking everything out with an eagle eye. Her eyes lit up when she saw the pile on the table.

I asked if she wanted tea, but she said, "No."

Her eyes never left the pile.

When I pointed at the table a smile that could light a tunnel spread across her face. She walked over and patted the pieces, deciding how to carry her load. Robert offered to help, but she firmly shook her head no.

First, she picked up a 20-pound bag of rice. With no trace of a grunt she whipped the bag up and onto her head. Next, she picked up a beautiful woven mat I had bought in Timbuktu. It was at least 6 feet wide and 10 feet long, and with no effort she placed the rolled mat on top of the bag of rice. When she felt confident with her balance she hoisted a large metal cook pot, loaded with onions, onto the mat placed on the bag of rice.

As she turned to go she smiled widely, and our eyes locked in mutual respect. It was hard to know who was happier — her, the recipient, or me, the giver. Shifting the load balanced on her head, she gave me a quick nod and bee-lined for the door. As she swept past she said in French, "I'm so glad I didn't hurt you!"

"I knew you could!" I shouted out in French and she laughed. The last I saw of her was the pile on her head walking by, swaying higher than the wall that divided and joined our separate worlds.

I HAD A SPLENDID TIME!
Venda, South Africa
2015

In 2015, at the age of 65, I met someone who touched me like no one has before. Vhuhwavho Nevhungoni, called Wavho or Woo, is the living example of confidence, courage, positive energy and commitment — and all at the age of 16.

Her story humbled me, her style amazed me, and her life inspired me beyond words. I had waited years to meet her, following her accomplishments, challenges and determination from afar through emails from her mom, Sue Anne Cook, and periodic news articles from the South African press. At last in June 2015, we met.

Her beautiful physical presence and peace of mind are obvious right away. Where others have kept silent, she has been vocal. Where others have been frightened, she has been brave. Where others have lived in fear, she has been bold.

Our connection was immediate and fun, and I just wanted to hug her non-stop. Together with her mom, Sue Anne, Joe, Woo and I, we traveled to a remote nature reserve called Leshiba, in the mountains of northeast South

Africa. For four days we talked and laughed and shared stories. And when we parted ways five days later I was dazzled. Accomplished beyond her years, and humble despite her contributions.

Woo was orphaned at two when her mother was taken by AIDS. Instead of being depressed or embarrassed as she grew up, she has been South Africa's, and possibly the world's, youngest AIDS/HIV activist, spanning 11 of her 16 years. She was lucky because her desperate grandmother knew she couldn't give Woo all the support she needed so she took her to a local clinic. There a Nursing Sister took her to my old friend, Sue Anne Cook. She had started a pre-school for AIDS orphans in her mobile home.

Sue Anne immediately took in the profoundly ill toddler, taking her to her doctor. Woo was diagnosed with Kwashiorkor and tuberculosis. Her ears were infected, and she had non-stop diarrhea.

"Also," added Sue Anne, "she didn't walk after being carried on her grandmother's back for a long time. The tests also confirmed that she was HIV positive. The doctor told me not to waste my money giving Woo antiretroviral (ARV) drugs, because she would never survive."

Fortunately, Sue Anne didn't follow that advice. It took

two years to clear-up Woo's malnutrition and tuberculosis, but her ears remained a problem. At the age of four, Woo started on her ARV drugs.

With the loving care of Sue Anne, Woo not only survived, but quickly learned as a four-year-old how to be solely responsible for taking her meds. She learned to measure the ARV syrups and knew which pills to take twice daily, timed with the 6 a.m. and 6 p.m. radio news.

By age five, local doctors were so impressed with her rapid improvement that clinics began to call her to come in to teach other kids, especially the reluctant ones, how to be independent and take responsibility for their own meds. This was just the beginning of Woo empowering other HIV positive children.

When she was six she did a television interview on La Familia TV in South Africa, fielding questions about her medication; what happens if she misses them; side effects, and what advice did she have for other kids. Her message was and still is simple but profound:

- Take your meds
- Eat healthy
- Don't stress

- Get and give lots of love

At nine, Woo made a video encouraging HIV positive pregnant women to take their ARV drugs to protect their fetuses. That year, she and Sue Anne were invited to Scotland where Woo did a presentation to hundreds of people at a service of the Church of Scotland in Greenock. Her topic was "Living Positively with HIV".

In 2007, based on Woo's success, Sue Anne and Woo started the first pediatric Anti Retro Viral support group for kids, of which Woo is still an integral and leading member. She did all these things and was recognized as an AIDS activist and speaker before she reached double digits. All of this out-reach work planted the seed for her future. Today Woo is an even busier activist (while attending high school), encouraging other kids not only to take their drugs, but to be responsible for them as soon as possible. Her second message is what she's most passionate about — don't be ashamed.

I was often speechless as she talked casually about some of the challenges she has faced. Woo is a strong and effective leader in the ARV support group she's been in since the age of seven. They started small — 12 members from 7 to 11-years-old. Their original focus was on the meds they needed to take and the consequences of failing to do so. From those days, they have grown to more than 150 kids in her small region in Venda, the northeast corner of South Africa. There are now four satellite support groups in other villages.

"We are closer than most families are. We have faced a lot and always supported one another. Now we share with new groups that help HIV positive kids be optimistic and supportive of one another."

As the original members get older they are taking over more of the leadership role of their group. They not only visit groups just getting started but show them that there is a "normal" life with AIDS.

"We know our support groups are helping because fewer kids are dying of AIDS. There's better attendance at workshops for meds training and better school attendance because the kids are healthier and stronger."

She said all this like someone telling you what they had for breakfast.

Fighting the stigma attached to AIDS is a main focus of the support groups. The stigma is particularly profound on kids, especially at the village level. The fear of being singled out is a major cause of kids defaulting on their drug regimes. Woo and Sue Anne noticed that kids often fell ill during or shortly after group trips with their schools or churches. They didn't want anyone to see them taking their meds and so defaulted, often with serious consequences. Woo's proud of her group.

"It's fun because we make plays and put them on for anyone who wants to watch. We're trying to help kids be brave. To own their HIV positive status."

Woo's support group creates workshops for other kids that go far beyond the original mandate of meds education. During one workshop, they wrote a play that they put on for the two nights at the game lodge where their workshop was being held.

"It was exciting," she said with a bright smile that competed with her shining eyes, "because participants, camp staff and tourists all came. Some more than once. The theme was to not just discourage kids from being ashamed, but to encourage them to actively educate others."

The workshops are important because they take kids to places they would never have an opportunity to visit otherwise, on a mini-vacation with a purpose. To be surrounded by other HIV positive kids gives them an idea of just how widespread the illness is and how many kids there are just like them.

As Woo says, "The workshops are fun with a social impact. It's a way of giving back to our community."

All her dedication to making a difference for her peers has not gone totally unnoticed. In 2011, at the age of 12, she was featured in the Natal Sunday Tribune as one of "Nine Inspirational South Africans Under 30" making a positive impact on society. She's been featured in uBuntu Magazine for all her contributions and is included in a Life Skills textbook for ninth graders as an example of a kid making a difference.

Recently she started a Facebook page called "A Life Worth Living" to give friends and strangers an outlet to share the challenges of life with HIV. She has also started a group chat two nights a week on a site called "What's Up?" She is regularly asked to speak at World AIDS Day ceremonies by hospitals and her school. She never says no.

Woo knows her illness so well and is so dedicated to getting the right information out that she corrected her teacher in science class who was unwittingly giving misinformation about AIDS. The teacher was not only surprised, but impressed, so she arranged for Woo to do a

Q&A session with the 12th graders at her school. It was the perfect environment for the students to freely ask questions of a peer and meet someone HIV positive who looks as healthy and happy as they are. It was a brave thing to do in a small high school. Woo is so vibrant that most people don't believe she is HIV positive. That's what positivity and responsibility can do.

And through this all Woo has dealt with her hearing problems. In 2010, an audiologist discovered that both eardrums had been badly perforated by the series of infections as a toddler. She had only 38 percent hearing in her right ear and 28 percent in her left. The Church of Scotland funded the necessary surgeries. A successful operation on her right ear restored 99.1 percent hearing with the implantation of a new eardrum. Unfortunately, the left ear was more damaged, and after three unsuccessful operations she is basically deaf in that ear. But you would never know it, and in true Woo fashion she consoled her mother, Sue Anne, saying, "It's not a big problem."

Her bravery and accomplishments are all thanks to her mother. I first met Sue Anne Cook in 1991 when she was visiting Mozambique. Sue Anne was the most under-the-radar person I had ever met. Her day jobs included delivering firewood and driving a school bus, and then living a quiet, unnoticed life. When the old grandmother brought Woo to the solitary white woman in her trailer, Sue Anne didn't hesitate for a second about changing her life to include a young HIV positive girl. And she never considered following the negative doctor's advice.

In 1993, entirely under her own steam and responding to the community's concerns about the growing number of AIDS orphans, Sue Anne converted her mobile home into two classrooms. Not only did she start a school, but she used her pickup truck as the school bus. Soon friends were donating furniture, toys and nutritional food. This was the start of Vhutshilo Mountain School, which opened in 2001. "Vhutshilo" means "life" in the local Tshivenda language.

As a result of Sue Anne's work, an old friend who had been a Peace Corps volunteer in South Africa, Jo Ann Churchill, and her friend Nancy Amanti, started Hope for Limpopo (http://www.hopeforlimpopo.org/), an amazing NGO. This organization supports the school.

Being surrounded by strong women created an inspiring and empowering environment, which accounts for who Woo is today. It's extremely rare to meet someone so dedicated, passionate, fearless and confident at such a young age. Woo, a child herself, has been an outspoken AIDS activist for three-fourths of her short life. It's hard to imagine the impact she will have as an adult. The one thing she knows for certain is that she will always be involved in HIV projects and programs.

It's impossible to know how many kids and adults Woo has impacted already. I am sure that with her dedication to educate and to encourage and empower through positivity and confidence, her impact will continue to be like the ripple from a pebble tossed in a pond — forever growing bigger.

In 2015 our trip into the bush included game drives looking for rhinos and hippos, elephants and giraffes. But Woo was the highlight for me. We talked and laughed and oohed and aahed at the great animals we saw. She did her accents for me, of Americans, French, Scots and Brits. She's a confident kid who likes to laugh and hug and share stories. And she's humble and hard-working, just doing what she needs to do — reaching out to others and empowering them by claiming her HIV status. Who knows how many HIV positive people, both kids and adults, will be inspired by this teenager in the future?

I thought the highpoint of the visit was our meeting

and connecting. But the real highlight came when she sent me an email to say, "I had a SPLENDID time with you!"

It doesn't get better than that.

CHATS ABOUT HATS
St. John, U.S. Virgin Islands
2015

In 2015, I was involved in a great program. The head of the St. John School of the Arts, Kim Wild, called and asked if I'd like to do a collaboration with the dance classes. I had no idea how that could happen, but I was immediately on-board.

Kim had recently seen a book about elderly women in the States, and their hats. She was intrigued by the idea of doing a different artistic expression of the same theme. I was to interview four matrons of St. John about their hats.

As a collector of hats from around the world I was in hog heaven. The final outcome was a wonderful program of dance set to music, with a reader telling shortened versions of the interviews. I still smile when I think of the celebration of matrons on St. John.

It didn't take long to set up interviews with the women, all of them in their 70s. They were all eager to talk, especially because hats are an integral part of their lives, but not something they could remember ever being discussed before. It was amazing how the topic of hats revealed so many things that had changed drastically on the island and in society, since they were kids on St. John. It was an honor for me to spend time with each woman. Dignified is the word that comes to mind when I think of these women.

Our conversations ranged over a wide range of topics, and one that kept repeating itself was about the younger generation.

"They just don't talk or enjoy family like we used to."

Another mentioned how they all are too busy looking at their phones.

"They aren't even talking on them, just writing messages."

Many times I heard a variation on, "I don't think that there is good communication between the generations."

Miss Childs was the first to meet me at the School of the Arts. She walked in the door and smiled a big hello. Her tall frame was formal and casual at the same time. A comfortable Panama hat adorned her head. Letting them each tell their stories in their own words will let you see the changes that have occurred, as well as the joy and pride they have in their hats.

Miss Childs:

I grew up in Cruz Bay until I was about 14. It was a village then, like a big family. We celebrated together and sympathized together as one family. If someone heard a child crying everyone came. They would take you on a walk or visit the bay with you.

I was still a small child when I got my first hat. Even before I started school. There was a woman who plaited hats from straw. She wove them like someone plaits hair. She plaited hats for girls going to school. For the little girls, they had a ribbon to tie under the chin, I think so they wouldn't fly off when we ran. Hats were always part of the back to school clothes. That lady made some fine styles with her hats.

Today I like to wear a hat with a wide brim, so I can wrap a scarf around it. I have many scarves and many hats. I wear the same ones a lot until I go to the back of the group and pull out something I haven't seen for a while. Sometimes I put it aside and sometimes I look at it and then just put it back. When I was up north I had hats with plumes or feathers, but not anymore. I like Panama hats because you can shape them. My hats for church are dressier.

Sometimes when I wear a hat it just makes me feel better. You can tilt it to match your mood. It says a little more about the way you are feeling. I usually wear a hat when I leave the house. It depends on my hairstyle. Usually I have a hat to protect me from the sun. Also, a hat does something special for me some time, so I like that. A nice hat can make you feel better, more together.

I'll never forget when I wore a hat to my first opera. I had it on to finish my outfit because I was dressing up. What I didn't know is that you aren't supposed to wear a hat to the opera. There was an older man mumbling behind me, but I didn't know it was about me until a young man tapped me on the shoulder and asked me to remove my hat. I did - and I never made that mistake again. It's hat etiquette.

We go on cruises now, and if I see someone wearing a fine hat some place we stop, I get one there. If I don't buy one my husband might ask, "Not getting a hat this time?" I got my Panama hat in Ecuador. It came rolled up in a small box, it is made so fine. And when I'm in New York if I see a hat store I go in and try hats on. If I'm in Macy's or Gimbels I go to their hats departments and try hats on.

Times change with generations. When I was growing up all girls and women wore hats. Not all women wear hats to church now. Young women will wear a hat to church sometime. So, I think that hats will always be around. Hats definitely have a future.

Miss Hill:

When I was growing up you would always see women wearing their hats. My mother used to say, "Women wear hats to church and men take them off." We had straw hats made by hand by a woman over in the BVI where I grew up.

I don't like big hats because I like to wear a hat down on my forehead — so I prefer little ones. Thin ones, not the wide, wide ones. When I do Worship Service on Sundays at church I don't wear a wide hat because I don't want people to look at the hat, I prefer them to listen to what I say. I don't want to wear one over my face, because that would like take away from what I'm saying. They'd be looking at that instead of listening.

I wouldn't say I have a lot of hats, but the ones I have are old. They don't fit so well because my hair is less full than it used to be. But every once in a while, I see them, love them and leave them. Now I can crochet some for myself. I learned to crochet from when I was young, but then a cousin taught me to read it recently and that helped me a lot because now I can take up a pattern and try to follow it. Maybe I don't get everything a 100 percent. I can make my own hats and I can read a pattern now.

I admire a woman that looks very nice. Some wear hats to match their clothes and that finishes the outfit. I look, and I say, "That person looks really nice." I feel more completely dressed with my hat on. Some places I go don't need a hat, but mostly at night with the weather I wear a hat to keep the cold off my head and in the day to keep sun off it, too.

Sometimes I watch different worship programs on TV, and some of the hats they wear are out of this world! I might be able to help someone if they put on a hat and asked me, I could say that one looks better than the other. For me I look in the mirror and if it's ok, I just wear it. I don't know any secrets about choosing a hat. I just look in the mirror.

Today is not like when we were growing up. Not so many hats, and sometimes not worn right. Pastor George says baseball caps on backwards are bad boy style or bad girl style. Not good. In church, I don't see so many hats, like when growing up, but I can tell you — I still like mine.

Miss Callwood:

I was about 10 years old when I got my first hat. My mother was in St. Thomas and she sent me and my sister nice white hats for Easter. It is a family tradition, wearing hats to church. You wear a hat to show respect for God in his house.

My grandmother never went to church unless she had her head covered. When I was growing up, if we didn't have a hat for church we wore a mantilla to cover our heads. My grandmother never kneeled to pray unless her head was covered with a mantilla, so it was a sacred something we did in our family. It's a tradition that was handed down to me from my parents and my grandparents.

I haven't passed this tradition on to my children because they think it's old fashioned, so they don't wear hats. But, they give me a hat for Christmas most every year. Some I have never worn because they don't fit my face. I have to fit the hat, no one can tell me what hat fits my face. I have more hats than I can count, stuffed in closets and boxes and bags.

The hats I wear most are custom made. I have my own hat maker on St. Thomas. She comes with hats and if I like one I say, "I'll take this one, but in a special color." When I was being honored at Frenchman's Reef I didn't have a hat for the night. I told her I needed a silver hat, to go with my outfit. She made a fine one.

Not all hats are right for me. I may not like the shape, and it has to match my face, or I don't wear it. I feel comfortable in a hat, like I am ready for whatever I am going to do. Without my hat on I am not ready to go. I feel like part of me is missing — the hat makes me complete. My image is very important to me, since I was a child, and I've passed this on to my children. There must be a difference between how you look at home and how you look outside. You don't need to be rich but be clean and neat.

There are not so many hats in church anymore. In fact, one Christmas a lady gave me a hat and I wore it to church and the minister mentioned my hat. He encouraged others to wear hats, and now they do. I have received many comments about my hats over the years. One lady asked me if there is any color hat I don't have, and I told her, "I don't think so."

Miss Blake:

A hat makes a statement. I have green, gold, tan, purple, red, white, black, and black and white hats. I love all my hats, but my favorite hat is this black and white one. My friend Millicent made it for me. She bought the hat plain, then added the lace and flowers and made this beautiful hat for me. The green rose hat is number two. It's the latest one that I got in Florida.

I probably wore my first hat when I was about 10. I grew up on Nevis and the British like to wear their hats, just like the Queen. I was an Anglican when I was there, and I was in the choir. We never, ever, went to church bare-headed; we had to wear a hat. I still do. I have been in the Virgin Islands for 67 years and eight months, and I am happy to see all the women in church with their hats. If I see a well-dressed woman, with a nice hat, I gawk at her — not look, but gawk — she looks so good.

You feel good when you have a dress, hat, shoes and bag that match. I pick the dress first, then choose the hat from a color or stripe or something in the dress. I love hats and shoes and I feel very confident when I am dressed up. I went to a funeral on St. Croix, and after, we went into a shop and the woman there said, "Oh my! Aren't you gorgeous! Look at that hat!" It's the same black and white hat that is my favorite one. It was good to have the woman appreciate my hat.

I have a sister named Elaine, who loves the hats, but not to wear. So, when she sees a nice hat she buys them for me, not herself. She would see a hat and say, "This looks just like Lena." And then give me that hat. My daughter bought me a dress and shoes to go with a hat I have.

A hat says something about the person wearing it. You can fit it just right, and tilt it or not, it is up to you. I prefer hats with rims and brims. I pick a color from the dress and match it up. I never lend my hats, no, no, no! I have many, and they are all well-preserved in the top of my closet.

I see lots of women, mainly my age, wearing hats in church. The younger women not so much, but the older women, yes. I love my hats!

Spending time with these women was an honor. They were enthusiastic, funny and frank. So frank that Miss Hill gave me a stern look and said, "Did you hear what I said about bad boy, bad girl style?"

Then she rested her eyes on my head. I am known on St. John for my backward baseball cap. I forgot that I was wearing it until that moment. Sheepishly, I removed it.

Years ago, I was at an evening event for Julius E. Sprauve School in Cruz Bay. Two elderly women were at our table and they had been looking at me like, "I know her but what's her name?"

Finally, one poked the other one who cleared her throat and said, "You must be dressed up because you don't have your backward cap on."

I clapped and laughed as I told Joe, "I have just lowered the dress-up bar so low that all I need to do is take off my cap!" YES! Which makes me love my hats, too!

AFTERWORD
St. John, USVI
2017

Thanks for taking this journey with me. I hope you have enjoyed this trip around the world, filled with amazing women. I find looking back on my life reminds me of two African proverbs. One is: "Life isn't about what you haven't done — it's about what you do next." And it's obvious to me that I need a new project.

The second proverb is: "If you go alone you'll go fast — but if you go together you'll go far." That's exactly what Joe and I have done. I'm thankful for the freedom that being an Ikut Swami has provided me, and I'm even more thankful for Joe. He has beat cancer twice, been through numerous heart procedures, and stayed by the side of Noise Patrol with a patience few have. I can't wait to see what the future holds...

AN AFTERWORD'S AFTERWORD
St. John, Virgin Islands
2018

Ten days after finishing Tales of an Ikut Swami, all hell broke loose in St. John and the Virgin Islands. Within 12 days we were ravaged by two Category 5 hurricanes — Irma hit on Sept. 6, and Maria on the 18th. Irma was the biggest hurricane to ever hit the Atlantic with sustained winds of 185-plus mph for eight solid hours. It also had gusts of over 270 mph, and we experienced it all. I started writing updates as a record of all the shocking changes that have become our "new normal."

I started this book revealing my Noise Patrol nickname. Remember that sound of a cricket, rooster or mad drumming that could drive me crazy? Well, those days are done.

I now thrive on the back-up beep of a truck, the sounds of buzz saws and of yelling men. They mean recovery, and electricity, which we haven't had for 13 weeks. There are over 700,000 cubic meters of vegetation debris, and 1.3 million cubic meters when the building debris is included. Chain saws mean clearing roads, removing debris, and progress. We won't have electricity for another five or six weeks if we depend totally on the local power company, WAPA (Water and Power Authority). Fortunately, we're maybe only two to three weeks from having power thanks to the solar panels we installed years ago. Just waiting for the Power Wall to arrive and be installed, then we'll have solar power. Yahoo!

It's great to have something to look forward to since every day is a challenge, and we are amongst the minority of people with minimal damage. Our little wooden house on stilts at 940 feet took a direct hit from Maria — and stayed intact. We lost a shutter, a plate glass door blew in but didn't break, our septic got messed up, the wind blew a supporting beam into our cistern and drove a bolt through it, our dart board cupboard was destroyed, the railing is missing pieces — and we were lucky.

I know lots of folks who lost everything, and close to half the permanent population has departed. We walked home the day after Irma after staying with our friends Dorothy and Fernando. It was a walk from hell — over huge piles of debris made of trees, mangrove, buildings, roofs, power poles, and a stream of shocked faces. It was like being in an apocalypse film, our faces as distressed and overwhelmed as all the faces we encountered.

Gov. Mapp announced the next night on the radio, "If you can't live without power, water, communication, TV, conveniences, then leave now. We don't need complainers. St. John has been thrashed and trashed and it's gonna take a long time to get back to 'normal.'"

He encouraged parents to send kids away because they were going to miss a lot of school this year on St. John. Again, he said, "Anyone who can't contribute needs to leave." I've seen many friends who have lost everything. We are so lucky, so humbled, and so grateful. And so sad.

It took two days to clear our driveway of trees and leaves so we could access it with a vehicle. Then it took two more days to clear the road from our driveway, to where Ajax Peak begins. Ajax Peak to Centerline Road, normally a 3-minute drive, also took days to clear, but we hired someone else to do that. And we are the lucky ones.

During all this drama we had another mini-drama when I took out the five stitches Joe had in his hand from a biopsy that had been done before Irma. That was a first for both of us.

Five days after Hurricane Irma, I fell on my knee replacement, off a 2-foot wall onto a paved driveway. The swelling was immediate, but I was lucky because our fridge was being powered by a neighbor's generator a few hours a day, so I had ice packs.

We went to the clinic the next day, after the 6 p.m. to noon curfew lifted. The clinic was a wreck and has since been condemned and closed. I sat in the doorway for light and air with a doctor and nurse with DEMAT, a medical emergency team from Colorado. The doctor said only an x-ray could determine if I had damaged the implant.

He also said I had a contusion under the knee cap that was a bruised deep purple and was bulging out the side of my knee cap. I spent eight days on two crutches and then 10 more on one crutch. Not the most convenient time to be on crutches. One of the best things that came out of it was I got a new nickname. Rupert, the deli guy at Starfish Market (who also wears a backward cap), told a long line of people, "I have to help Cris on a Crutch first."

Then there was the drama of breaking a back molar in half while grinding my teeth during my sleep. Or maybe I did it during Maria, when we went to the giant cement house above us and I sat in a closet from 2:00 a.m. to 6:30 a.m. Joe brought the only chair in the room into the closet for me because I couldn't take the furious sounds of the wind wrapping around the front and side walls of the room we were tucked into.

I never felt at physical risk, for the house is a cement fortress. What got to me was the audible definition of rage, the sound of fury. Maria, the second Cat 5, went on for 12 hours, through the night. Darkness magnified the intensity of wind and rain and sound.

Irma had been during the day, and at one point I was looking out a tiny bathroom window that had lost its shutter. It looked out on the backside of our friends' house, at the driveway, and suddenly a tall, broken tree flew in. A double mattress followed that, and then a surfboard arrived.

Seeing the madness was better than being battered by the sounds in the darkness. Maria went on and on in the black night lit only by frequent jagged lightning bolts, for more than 12 long, nerve-racking hours. It formed a double eyewall during its peak, something not seen before. We were in the bull's eye. As I sat in the tiny walk-in closet, I could see the lightning flashes in the crack on the shutter opposite the closet. No wonder I'm still on the thin edge of the wedge...

And during all this madness some sweet moments

popped up, and they all involved local women. The first happened on the ferry, coming back from St. Thomas after getting my x-rays. I had to wait for two weeks after my fall for x-rays on my knee.

The building that had the machine was being repaired, and actually two weeks was very fast! The x-rays were good news, showing no indication of damage to my titanium knee.

It was on my return trip that a woman came up to me on the ferry. I didn't recognize her, and still don't know who she is, but she put the first smile on my face in weeks.

We were just pulling away from the dock on St. Thomas when she sat beside me and said, "I am so happy to see you with your backward baseball cap on. It makes me feel normal."

She could see my amazement and joy, then said, "So thanks, my dear. Normal is good."

She patted my knee then scooted down the bench to talk with a friend across the aisle.

While waiting to get off, I told her, "Thanks for telling me that. I don't know why I didn't wear it for a while. But now I'm really glad I have it back on."

Then as an afterthought I said, "How did you know I usually wear one?"

"I see," she said, "I see." When we parted ways, I was smiling like I hadn't in weeks. It was also my first day without crutches, so the best day since Sept. 12th, five days after Irma hit.

And then I remembered Miss Hill in the group of women telling me about their hats. She had told me my backward cap represented a bad boy, bad girl persona. That had me more determined to wear my backward cap, but the good vibes from my new ferry friend makes me even more determined never to leave home without it. It just proves that good overpowers negative.

Six weeks after Hurricane Irma we got on a plane to Paris. We had a trip planned for months to go to a friend's wedding in Brittany. The trip almost didn't happen. The airport on St. Thomas was in an emergency repair state, working on the aftermath shambles of the storms.

American Airlines cancelled our flight, claiming that they had called and emailed. Only we didn't have access to either thing. We eventually left on Delta, but I didn't believe it would happen until I was in my seat. As we took off I breathed a huge sigh of relief, and Joe took my hand.

Going from hurricane-ravaged St. John to rural France was like jumping on a rocket ship and changing planets. Brittany was beautiful, with tall green trees, cold sharp air, and no destroyed buildings. I spent most of the 10 days sitting by and tending a roaring fire. The wedding, and all its variety of activities, was a little overwhelming, as I wasn't really in a social mood. But it was a great break from our small destroyed island.

A few weeks after our return home from France another disaster struck. If dealing with my knee wasn't enough, I complicated things by having to have a tooth pulled. I woke on a Tuesday with a slight toothache. By Wednesday, the pain was out of control, and so on Thursday, I got on a ferry to St. Thomas and took a taxi most of the way to the dentist in the middle of the island.

The traffic was so terrible with all the debris in the roads and crews working that I finally just jumped out of the cab and walked the rest of the way — uphill in a scorching sun. When I unexpectantly arrived in the dentist's office, sweating like Niagara Falls, face as red as a ripe strawberry, contorted in pain, the receptionists were shocked and concerned.

I was in a dental chair within five minutes, obviously in

serious pain and desperate enough to just gate crash their office. The dentist was great, although he was also shocked by my sudden arrival and scary appearance. A few numbing shots later he announced that I needed to have the tooth pulled.

I was distraught. He then ground it down, so it didn't hit any other teeth. I left in shock, walked back to the road and waited in the sun for another 20 minutes until a dollar taxi appeared. Traffic flow was sporadic as flag crews controlled who went in what direction at any given moment. I told Joe that night that if I had seen me on the roadside I would probably have passed by, too — for being way too scary looking.

On my wait at the ferry terminal on St. Thomas, discouraged and in shock, another woman lifted me from my gloom. She had her hair piled high on her head, and lots of gold bling on her wrists. Her deep chocolate skin didn't have a wrinkle, although I was pretty sure she was my age.

She kept glancing my way, and I wondered if my shorts that used to be too snug had dropped too low or something, as not eating for weeks had caused a weight loss that had reached 14 pounds.

Her repeated looks were finally explained when she pointed to my arm and said, "I'm so happy to see that beautiful African bracelet again."

I normally wear a beautiful wide black, red and white beaded bracelet. It's as much a part of me as my backward baseball cap. But during my 18 days on two, then one crutch, I couldn't wear my bracelet. Off crutches, the bracelet was back on.

Like the cap lady, she said, "It makes things more normal."

And once again, her friendly outreach made me forget briefly the total devastation of our beautiful little island. And the numerous friends I had run into that had lost everything. Of the destruction of Joe's Friends of the Park office, and the exhausting day spent moving from there to a much smaller, but safe, dry and electrified space.

And through all the emotional turmoil of viewing destruction daily, the woman mentioning my bracelet brought the second big St. John smile to my face. We were eight weeks into no electricity, roads lined with huge piles of debris, sadness and a tough community showing lots of grit. That comment about my bracelet, from a total stranger, broke my funk.

That night I told Joe, "I feel like I'm not nearly under the radar like I thought. Two women have commented on my style, or lack thereof, so I must not be totally invisible like I thought I was."

And through it all I was anticipating my tooth pull. It was a five-day wait for the pulling, so my diet of soup, yoghurt and mashed potatoes had made me another 2 pounds lighter — and, boy, did that make my knee happier.

Getting the tooth pulled was easier than the five-day wait. Joe took me and brought me back, which was still a long afternoon, taking four hours to get back to St. John after waiting for a barge.

But then another little miracle happened as the barge we were sure we wouldn't make took us on at the last moment. Maybe the woman loading the barge could sense my pain and despair at the thought of waiting another 90 minutes. All I know is that she suddenly turned and waved us on. We finally got home, and it was back to the ice packs.

But still the dental drama wasn't over. It was like my mouth went into protest, and the next thing I knew I needed a deep cleaning because the gums were infected. I couldn't believe it, and tears poured down my face. It was embarrassing because we still had a house, and a generator, and a functioning fridge, and yet there I was playing the pity game.

The next day another woman I didn't know told me, "You sure are looking good."

Tilting her head full of tight grey braids adorning her scalp she said, "You have a nice color and look fit."

That was thanks to the 16 pounds I had lost at that point due to the dental challenges. In that moment I realized the opportunity I had to lose that 20 pounds I had planned to lose for months, maybe even years. With a 16-pound head start I could take advantage of the weight loss, or not. But it was my new friend that had spoken a spontaneous comment about my appearance that gave me the determination to carry on purposefully to lose those next four pounds.

Again, a woman I didn't know, but obviously had seen before, spurred me onto a new positive decision.

"Women do that for each other," I told Joe that night.

And while I was making these decisions, arguments raged in the bigger picture about the governor wanting to set fire to the 700,000 cubic yards of vegetation debris.

Ecology groups, health experts around the states and

local environmental groups fought against it.

National and local environmental groups are strongly fighting the burning option, saying the smoke could cause many health problems. One tree, the manchineel, also known as the "death apple" for its extreme toxicity, can cause severe respiratory distress and irritation of skin and eyes. The health and ecological groups want to chip and compost, which would be a massive amount of stuff, but safer.

Thirteen medical and public health officials from across the states have written to Gov. Mapp discouraging the burning of debris. Let's hope sanity wins out on this one, but doubtful since he announced he will burn 35% of it starting Friday of this week. Still hoping for the best.

And through all of this madness another woman brought big smiles to Joe's and my faces. We were shopping in town when this lovely West Indian woman, as tall as me and easily my age, but very stylish, tapped me on the shoulder. When I turned to greet her she said, "Every time I see you I think of twiga."

Joe and I were both very surprised, because twiga is Swahili for giraffe. I asked why, and she said, "Fifteen years ago I taught at Sprauve. You came in and did your Power

Point presentation of Africa and told us about the day that seven silent giraffes surrounded you, munching on the trees you were sitting under, and they stayed for a few hours."

Shaking her head, she said, "I never forgot it because I had never seen those kids so quiet. And when you left, twigas are all they talked about for days. It became their favorite animal, too." Patting my arm again she said, "And so when I see you, I think twiga."

I gave her a big hug and said, "You have no idea how happy I am you told me this. I still love twigas and now I love you too!"

We both laughed and once again, a woman's kindness to tell me something totally unexpected gave me a boost out of the hurricane brain syndrome we are all experiencing here.

On the day I went to have the deep cleaning of my gums, I arrived at the dentist and told him as soon as he came in, "I don't think I need this. My gums are feeling fine after 10 days of antibiotics, and my dental hygiene has improved significantly."

He laughed and said, "It's all part of the process. We've prepared and now we'll finish the job."

I wasn't happy, but what were the choices? When he

finished and left the room, his dental assistant told me, "You know I never speak up for myself. What you did is what I need to start doing. My generator isn't working, and I can't even figure out where the dipstick is. And my 24-year-old son is no help."

Not really knowing for sure about the dipstick, I said, "Look on the side for a little ringy thing on a wire. That should be a dipstick."

As I got up to leave she said, "Myself, I'm about ready to give up."

I hugged her and said, "Please don't do that. Get your son to help you."

With a smile suddenly creeping across her face she said, "You know, you're right. I need to tell him what I need instead of hoping he figures it out. I just can't stay silent. I need to speak up for myself just like you did. You've inspired me, and I'm telling him tonight to man up!"

And that's what women do for each other. We encourage, inspire, support, and hug.

So, thank you, Joe, for encouraging me to be an independent Ikut Swami. It's led me down all kinds of unexpected paths, and into projects that I never knew I could or would do.

And the bottom line is, if Crusieamatic Cristina can do it, anyone can! Women are powerful, and as an African saying goes, "Women working together can do anything."

And we do!

THE END

FRONT COVER PHOTOGRAPHY GUIDE

Top 1st row from left:

Ha'apai women, Tonga; Dianne Warren, Shitaye Astawes, Cristina, Rahel Mekuria, WOW Project, Ethiopia; Village woman, Bangladesh; Puel woman, Mali.

Top 2nd row from left:

Ingal Tuareg woman, Niger; Woo, Cape Town, South Africa; Dogon women, Mali.

Bottom 2nd row from left:

North Kordofan woman, Sudan; Karen Jones Meadows, Actor, US; Miss Childs, St. John, US Virgin Islands; North Kordofan girl, Sudan; Puel woman, Mali.

Bottom 1st row from left:

Sasak woman, Lombok, Indonesia; Samburu girl, Kenya; Maradi woman, Niger; Veve Jacobsen, Niue, South Pacific; Addis Ababa woman, Ethiopia; Carnival dancer, St. Thomas, US Virgin Islands.

To learn more about Cristina Kessler, visit her website:
www.cristinakessler.com

Made in the USA
Columbia, SC
26 November 2018